Corporate Acquisitions and Mergers in Indonesia

Corporate Acquisitions and Mergers in Indonesia

Second Edition

M. Idwan Ganie
Arum Tarina

Lubis Ganie Surowidjojo Law Firm

This book was originally published as a chapter in Corporate Acquisitions and Mergers.

General Editor: Peter Begg

Wolters Kluwer

Published by:
Kluwer Law International B.V.
PO Box 316
2400 AH Alphen aan den Rijn
The Netherlands
E-mail: international-sales@wolterskluwer.com
Website: lrus.wolterskluwer.com

Sold and distributed in North, Central and South America by:
Wolters Kluwer Legal & Regulatory U.S.
7201 McKinney Circle
Frederick, MD 21704
United States of America
Email: customer.service@wolterskluwer.com

Sold and distributed in all other countries by:
Air Business Subscriptions
Rockwood House
Haywards Heath
West Sussex
RH16 3DH
United Kingdom
Email: international-customerservice@wolterskluwer.com

Printed on acid-free paper

ISBN 978-94-035-0854-2

e-Book: ISBN 978-94-035-0855-9
web-PDF: ISBN 978-94-035-0860-3

This title is available on www.kluwerlawonline.com

Printed in the United Kingdom.

Lubis Ganie Surowidjojo Law Firm

In our more than thirty years of service, we have secured our position as the premier Indonesian corporate transaction and commercial litigation law firm. We have over a hundred lawyers and experience representing a diverse range of clients, including domestic and multinational corporations, public and private companies, Government instrumentalities, and State Owned Enterprises. We work closely with our clients to understand their problems, determine their needs, and arrive at practical solutions that are both cost-effective and viable over the long term.

We strive to understand a client's needs and the legal complexities faced by them in Indonesia's highly dynamic legal and business landscape, translate this into a solution, and then see the successful outcome. To this end, we approach our clients' assignments with a pragmatic view that is driven by a deep understanding of their business needs and of the surrounding practicalities of the legal and business landscape that they operate in.

Representative Clients

Adaro Indonesia; American Bureau of Shipping; Astra International; Astratel Nusantara; Bank Mandiri; Charoen Pokphand Indonesia; DBS Bank Ltd; Goldman Sachs; Hitachi; Hutchison (Hong Kong); Indonesia Infrastructure Guarantee Fund; Indonesian State Electricity Company (PLN); Japan Tobacco International Indonesia; Krakatau Steel; Liga Primer Indonesia (LPI); Medco Energi International; Ministry of Finance of the Republic of Indonesia; Mitsui & Co., Ltd; Mitsui Banking Corporation; Mitsui Indonesia; Pamapersada Nusantara; Sampoerna Strategic; Sime Darby (Malaysia); Simpson, Spence & Young (SSY); Standard Chartered Bank; Sumitomo; Temasek Holdings (Private) Limited; and Unilever Indonesia.

ISO

LGS has obtained Lloyd's Register Quality Assurance certifications of ISO 9001:2015 for Quality Management systems and ISO 14001:2015 for Environmental Management systems to ensure that all aspects of the firm's operations and the quality of services are on par with the most well managed companies and organizations in the world.

Practice Areas
- ADR and Arbitration
- Antitrust
- Bank and Debt Restructuring
- Banking and Secured Transactions
- Bankruptcy
- Capital Markets
- Construction
- Consumer Protection Defence Litigation
- Corporate Finance
- Distribution of Goods and Services

- E-commerce
- Energy
- Foreign and Domestic Investment
- Forestry and Plantations
- General Corporate
- Information Technology
- Infrastructure
- Insurance
- Intellectual Property Rights
- International Trade
- Labour
- Maritime and Shipping
- Mergers and Acquisitions
- Mining, Oil, and Gas
- Privatization
- Project Finance
- Property and Real Estate
- Refinancing and Bank Lending
- Shariah Transactions
- Structured Finance
- Telecommunications

Contact Details

Dr Mohamed Idwan ('Kiki') Ganie

Managing Partner

Lubis Ganie Surowidjojo

Menara Imperium 30th Floor

Jl. H. R. Rasuna Said Kav. 1 Kuningan

Jakarta 12980, Indonesia

Tel.: +62 21 831-5005, 831-5025

Fax: +62 21 831-5015, 831-5018

E-mail: ganie@lgslaw.co.id

Website: www.lgsonline.com

Authors

Dr M. Idwan Ganie, SH

Mohamed Idwan ('Kiki') Ganie is the Managing Partner of Lubis Ganie Surowidjojo, one of Indonesia's largest law firms, which he co-founded in 1985. He graduated from the Faculty of Law of the University of Indonesia and holds a Phd in Law from the University of Hamburg. Dr Ganie has completed further studies at the Institute for Advanced Legal Studies in London; the Max Planck Institute for International Private Law in Hamburg, Germany; and in political studies at the *Staatswissenschaftliche Fakultaet* of the University of Zurich. He is a licensed Indonesian capital market lawyer and a member of the Asia Pacific Bar Association.

Dr Ganie has more than thirty years of legal experience, and specializes in commercial transactions and commercial litigation, including alternative dispute resolution and has acted as an expert in a number of court and arbitration proceedings. His expertise covers general corporate/company law, banking law, finance (including lease finance), mining, investment, acquisitions, infrastructure projects/project finance, antitrust, and shipping/aviation, with a particular focus on corporate governance and compliance.

His international commercial transaction and litigation clients include: Goldman Sachs (US), Temasek Holdings (Singapore), Hutchison Whampoa (Hong Kong), and Mitsui (Japan).

He is a senior lecturer at the Faculty of Law at the University of Indonesia, a lecturer for the Indonesian Bar Association (PERADI), and a frequent speaker at international conferences and seminars covering a range of Indonesian legal issues. His publications include works on such topics as mining, shipping, finance, and dispute settlement.

Dr Ganie is a chairman of the Association of Indonesian Antitrust Lawyers, a member of the regional panel of the Singapore International Arbitration Centre (SIAC), a fellow (FSIarb) of the Singapore Institute of Arbitrators, and a member of the Association for International Arbitration (AIA).

He speaks Indonesian, English, German, and Dutch.

Arum Tarina, SH, LL.M.

Ms. Arum Tarina is a Lawyer at Lubis Ganie Surowidjojo. She graduated from the Faculty of Law, University of Indonesia, majoring in Business Law. During her university studies, she received honours as a Leading Student in National Human Rights and Corruption Moot Court Competition for three consecutive years. Prior joining Lubis Ganie Surowidjojo she has worked in-house and with another Jakarta-based law firm. She holds a license as an advocate from Peradi. Her practice includes competition law, technology law, investment law, corporate law, and commercial litigation. In 2012 she concluded her studies at Tilburg University, the Netherlands, earning a Master of Laws degree (LL.M.) in law and technology. She speaks Indonesian and English.

Contents

LOCAL ECONOMIC, POLITICAL, AND CULTURAL ASPECTS

[01] Indonesian civil law, including its commercial law, was inherited from the Dutch and adopted at the time of Indonesia's independence. Dutch civil law is derived from the French Code Civil and the latter is historically and conceptually derived from Roman law.

[02] The main form of business entity (the only form of legal entity whose capital is divided into shares) is the limited liability company (*Perseroan Terbatas* abbreviated '*PT*') – a corporate entity whose capital is divided into shares and with the personal liability of its shareholders limited to the amount of the shares subscribed by them. The PT is managed by a two-tier system comprising a board of directors (consisting of one or more members) charged with its day-to-day management under the supervision of a board of '*komisaris*'/commissioners (consisting of one or more members). The PT was initially regulated in the Commercial Code inherited from the Dutch and in its authentic Dutch text was referred to as '*Naamloze Vennootschap*' (*NV*); in form and substance it is almost identical to the old form of NV applicable in the Netherlands prior to the Dutch law reform which resulted in a distinction between NVs and BVs.

[03] In 1995 Indonesia promulgated its own law on the PT ('*Law No. 1/1995*') to substitute the section in the Indonesian Commercial Code dealing with PT(s). By virtue of the promulgation of such law, the provisions on PT in the Commercial Code are no longer applicable.

[04] The Law No. 1/1995 on PT does not make changes to the basic legal concept of PT and, among other things, introduces streamlined incorporation procedures and different classes of shares, incorporates stricter provisions for payment of share capital and protection of minority shareholders, and introduces provisions on mergers and acquisitions (previously governed under the Indonesian Commercial Code).

[05] On 16 August 2007, the Government promulgated Law Number 40 of 2007 on PT ('*Law No. 40/2007*' or the '*Company Law*'), which replaced Law No. 1/1995 as the previous law on PT. This new law set out new provisions on, among other issues, mergers, consolidations, and acquisitions, separation or spin-off policy, and obligation for a company whose business concerns the field of, or is connected with, natural resources to carry out its social and environmental responsibility.

[06] In various sectors the government has issued special provisions on mergers and acquisitions relevant only to specific industries, mostly of a procedural and technical nature.

[07] Separate regulations under the tax laws do not necessarily mirror the legal and accounting impact of a merger under the Company Law and Indonesian accounting principles but are primarily tax oriented. Other non-industry specific regulations have added legal uncertainty or administrative complexity, to say the least. Examples are the new antitrust regulations requiring approval for mergers and acquisitions from a special Antitrust Supervisory Commission and new labour regulations requiring significant compensation to employees in cases of mergers and acquisitions, even if the relevant employee does not forfeit employment and remains employed (admittedly, in certain cases, by a new employer from a legal point of view).

[08] Starting 2017, the Government aims to integrate the licensing system for the purpose of acceleration of doing business in Indonesia. The goal would be a 'one-stop service' and that legal implications would be deemed implemented by operation of law rather than requiring further implementing steps which in turn contain the risk of rejection (in the case of approval needed to transfer certain assets notwithstanding the merger) and potentially rendering the commercial objectives of the merger or acquisition impossible.

[09] In view of the above, it is difficult to determine positive progress in a merger transaction until the very last step has been completed. The smooth implementation of a proposed merger or acquisition will therefore largely depend on good coordination in order to overcome 'programmed' obstacles and the risk of failure at the very end or at best the risk of a high tax bill.

Politics and Culture

[10] Indonesia is a large and spread out archipelagic state with population and majority of development generally concentrated on the Java Island. However, natural resources on Sumatra, Kalimantan (Borneo), and Papua are playing increasingly important roles in the Indonesian economy and politics. In this respect, there has been a certain degree of resource nationalism that has at times resulted in what can be viewed as protectionist policies towards the natural resource sector. At the same time, the government fully realizes that the outlying islands severely lack much-needed infrastructure, and such development is often only possible through foreign investment.

[11] Except for such protectionist tendencies, that generally affect populist issues such as natural resources or traditional business sectors, Indonesia has a vibrant democracy and a reasonably developed legal system. An issue that has unfortunately been persistent for a number of decades in Indonesia is the level of corruption, which generally affects government officials and courts, particularly at first and second instance.

[12] In certain sectors, particularly those likely to be exposed to significant regulatory overhead and/or a history of corrupt practices the valuation expectations of vendors can be entirely unrealistic due to a combination of a view that it is impossible for an outsider to secure the assets/licenses that they hold and often the fact that the assets/licenses were secured by the owners at minimal cost, resulting in little downside to holding out for a future potential transaction (this is particularly true of mineral concessions). Additionally, and generally, silent partners are a prevalent feature in certain sectors, resulting in agreement for a transaction having to be secured not only from the actual shareholders of the target but also from 'stakeholders' who have influence over the shareholders.

Special Provisions

Special Provisions for the Banking Sector

[13] Mergers and acquisitions in Indonesia historically started in the banking and insurance sector. Because of a lack of general provisions in the Commercial Code, the Government at that time issued special regulations on mergers and acquisitions of banks (applicable only to the banking sector), with slight improvements and adjustments required to comply with Law No. 40/2007, which is still applicable today.

[14] Banking in general is regulated under Law Number 7 of 1992 as further amended with Law Number 10 of 1998 on Banking, while special provision on mergers and acquisition of bank is regulated under the Government Regulation Number 28 of 1999 on Mergers, Consolidation, and Acquisitions of Bank.

[15] The Financial Services Authority (*'Otoritas Jasa Keuangan'* or *'OJK'*), as the supervisor of financial institutions, has also issued Regulation No. 39/POJK.03/2017 on Single Ownership in the Indonesian Banking Sector, which provides a single presence policy of Indonesian banking limiting a party to become a controller of only one local bank, except for: (i) controlling shareholder in two banks that carry out business under a different principle, namely conventional and Shariah-based principles; and (ii) controlling shareholder in two banks, one of which is a Joint Venture Bank (as will be described below).

[16] Based on the regulation, a party is deemed a controlling shareholder if: (i) it holds 25% or more of shares of a company or a bank and owns voting rights; or (ii) it holds less than 25% of shares of a bank but owns voting rights and has evidently exercised control over the bank, either directly or indirectly. A party who has become the controlling shareholder in more than one bank or who purchased other bank's shares thereby becoming the controlling shareholder in more than one bank is required to adjust its ownership structure as follows:

(a) to implement a merger or consolidation on banks under its control;
(b) to form a Bank Holding Company by: (i) establishing a new legal entity as the Bank Holding Company; or (ii) appointing one of the banks under its control as the Bank Holding Company; or
(c) to establish a holding function. Holding Function is a function owned by controlling shareholder, in the form of Indonesian Bank or Indonesian Government, to consolidate and directly control its subsidiaries' all activities.

[17] The adjustment to ownership structure as set out in this OJK Regulation was required to be completed by:

(a) for the first two restructuring options, i.e., merger and establishment of a holding Bank Holding Company, the act must be implemented within one year after the execution of the purchase on other bank's shares and causes them meet criteria as controlling shareholders of the bank they purchased;
(b) for the establishment of a holding function, the act must be carried out within six months after the execution of the purchase on other bank's shares and causes them meet criteria as controlling shareholders of the bank they purchased.

[18] New regulations on bank ownership have been issued, the OJK Regulation No. 56/POJK.03/2016 on Share Ownership in Commercial Banks, restricting bank ownership to 20% for individuals, 30% for legal entities, and 40% for financial institutions, with above 40% ownership being permissible upon the fulfilment of certain requirements and following a certain period. This makes acquisitions of banks significantly more challenging, with the example of the acquisition by DBS of Bank Danamon, in 2013, which was ultimately abandoned after failing to secure regulatory approval within a reasonable time. More broadly, the regulation governing foreign investment (any shareholding and transactions by foreigners except in relation to listed companies) has been revised, slightly modifying the approval procedures that have to be carried out prior to the share transfer.

Special Provisions for Companies Operating under Foreign or Domestic Investment Laws

[19] On 26 April 2007, the Government promulgated the law on investment, Number 25 of 2007 on Investment (*'Law No. 25/2007' or 'Investment Law'*). In order to perform Ease of Doing Business principle (*'EoDB'*), the Government issued the new Government Regulation Number 24 of 2018 on Electronic Single Submission System (known as *'Online Single Submission'* or *'OSS'*) (*'GR No. 24/2018'*) that introduces an online based system for issuing certain business licenses. The implementing regulations by the Investment Coordinating Board (*'Badan Koordinasi Penanaman Modal'* or *'BKPM'*), are (i) the Head of Investment Coordinating Board Regulation Number 6 of 2018 on the Guidelines and Procedures for the Implementation of Capital Investment Licensing and Facilities (*'BKPM Regulation No. 6/2018'*); (ii) the Head of Investment Coordinating Board Regulation Number 7 of 2018 on the Guidelines and Procedure for Capital Investment Supervision (*'BKPM Regulation No. 7/2018'*), as well as the restrictions on investment as stipulated under the Presidential Regulation No. 44 of 2016 on the List of Business Fields that are Closed to and Business Fields that are Open with Conditions to Investment (known as the Indonesian *'Negative Investment List'/Daftar Negatif Investasi (DNI)*) (*'PR No. 44/2016'*). However, any corporate actions undertaken by any investment company that will involve the amendment of its articles of association or its company information (i.e., mergers, acquisitions, transfers of shares, and changes of corporate information) will not be managed by the OSS System. To the extent required by law/regulation, such action can be done only after obtaining required approvals or receipts from other relevant government authorities (e.g., the Ministry of Law and

Human Rights). The companies' information in the OSS System must be updated by the relevant companies after the completion of the corporate actions.

[20] Under BKPM Regulation No. 6/2018, a domestic company is subject to Business License application using Electronic Investment Service and Investment Licensing System/*Sistem Pelayanan Informasi dan Perizinan Investasi Secara Elektronik* ('*Online SPIPISE*'), while GR No. 24/2018 stipulates that the prevailing system would be the OSS System. Furthermore, Online SPIPISE is an application under supervision of BKPM built to serve investors in filing the licensing process for the implementation of investment activities in the territory of the Republic of Indonesia. Beside Online SPIPISE, the Indonesian Government launched the OSS that also serves investors related to licensing process starting from 8 July 2018. The OSS System issues business licenses which were given on behalf of Government Institution, Governor, or Regent/Mayor by an integrated electronic system. All foreign investments must be processed through either the OSS or the Online SPIPISE based on their respective business fields. After carrying out the registration with the OSS System, each business entity will obtain Business Identification Number ('*Nomor Induk Berusaha*' or '*NIB*') as it will also be featured with an electronic signature. Further, the minimum investment for foreign investments under BKPM Regulation No. 6/2018 are as set out below:

(a) A minimum investment of above IDR10 billion (excluding investment for land and buildings, except for the line of business related to property business and development) only applies for foreign investment companies and applies for one line of business in the same subclass business pursuant to Indonesian Standard Industrial Classification ('*KBLI*') and one project location in one region/municipal.
(b) The minimum investment for an expansion of business with the same line of business and the same project location can be less than IDR10 billion (excluding investment for land and buildings), provided that the total investment for that line of business and that project location must be above IDR10 billion (excluding investment for land and buildings), for: (i) project expansion of one business in one business group pursuant to KBLI in the same location; or (ii) expansion of one or more business in one subclass business pursuant to KBLI, that is not receive facility or receive facility outside Industry sector, in one location in one region/municipal.

[21] In addition, under BKPM Regulation No. 6/2018, foreign investment companies shall comply with the provision regarding the minimum issued and paid up capital of IDR2 500 000 000. All foreign investment must assume the form of a limited liability company ('*Perseroan Terbatas*' *or* '*PT*'), with the exception of investment in certain sectors (e.g., Banking and Oil & Gas, which can presently also operate through branches and representative offices, respectively).

[22] Under BKPM Regulation No. 6/2018, foreign investment companies can apply for a business licenses through the Online SPIPISE for certain business fields. BKPM through the Online SPIPISE remained authorized to issue business licenses in the energy and mineral resources sector; public works and housing sector; and also to process the applications for Foreign Company Representative Office (*'KPPA'*), branch opening licenses, recommendation for Limited Stay Visa (*'VITAS'*), recommendation for changing a Visit Stay Permit into a Temporary Stay Permit (*'ITAS'*), and recommendation for changing an ITAS to Permanent Stay Permit (*'ITAP'*). While other types of business licenses pursuant to GR No. 24/2018 are processed through OSS.

[23] The limits on foreign capital ownership that are set out in PR No. 44/2016 also apply to mergers, acquisitions, and consolidations. Therefore, the resulting foreign shareholding in the surviving company, the acquiring company, or the consolidated company will be subject to the enumerated ownership limits.

Special Provisions for Public Companies

[24] The third wave of mergers and acquisitions took place involving public companies after the reformation of the Indonesian capital market in the 1980s. Law Number 8 of 1995 on Capital Market (*'Law No. 8/1995'*) enables special regulations on mergers and acquisitions to be issued by regulating bodies for public companies, resulting in special regulations on mergers and acquisitions issued by the Capital Market and Financial Institution Supervisory Agency (*'BAPEPAM & LK'*) now called the Financial Services Authority (*'Otoritas Jasa Keuangan'* or *'OJK'*). Although BAPEPAM & LK was replaced by the OJK, all prevailing BAPEPAM & LK regulations remain in force until replaced or revoked.

[25] Mergers and acquisitions of public companies are specifically regulated under: (i) OJK Regulation No. 54/POJK.04/2015 on Voluntary Tender Offers; (ii) OJK Regulation No. 74/POJK.04/2016 on Merger or Consolidation of Public Companies as lastly amended by OJK Regulation No. 58/POJK.04/2017 on the Electronic Submission of Registration Statements and Applications for Corporate Actions; and (iii) OJK Regulation No. 9/POJK.04/2018 on Takeover of Public Company.

THE REGULATORY FRAMEWORK

Business Vehicles

[26] In Indonesia, the most common form of business vehicle is PT. PT is divided into two types, private and public companies. A private company is a legal entity that constitutes an alliance of capital established pursuant to a contract in order to carry on business activities with an authorized capital all of which is divided into shares, meanwhile public company is a company whose shares are owned by at least 300 shareholders with a capital of at least IDR3 000 000 000, or a number of shareholders and paid up capital stipulated by specific Government Regulation.

[27] To carry out business in Indonesia, foreign investment must be in the form of a PT, with the requirements to establish a PT set out in Law No. 40/2007. However, since shareholders are foreign, the regulations dealing with large-scale and foreign investment also apply. Pursuant to BKPM Regulation No. 6/2018 the required total investment value has to be more than IDR10 000 000 000 excluding any immovable assets (land and buildings). The paid-up capital has to be at least IDR2 500 000 000 and the value held by each shareholder has to be at least IDR10 000 000.

[28] The structure of PT is two-tier system comprising of a board of directors charged with its day-to-day management, which is supervised by a board of commissioners. Based on Law No. 40/2007, board of directors may consists of one or more members, and in case it consists of two or more members, the division of management tasks and authority between the members is determined in resolutions of the General Meeting of Shareholders ('*GMS*'), and one of the members is appointed as a president director. Sectoral regulations may require a specific number of directors and their respective qualifications.

[29] Unlike the Anglo-Saxon system, there is no such position as non-executive directors. The duty to supervise the board of directors is vested on the board of commissioners, which is tasked with the supervision of the company policies, the general management of the company and its business, as well as advising the board of directors.

[30] The board of directors shall represent company in and out of the courts as well as bear the responsibility for the management of the company. Except as stipulated otherwise in the company's articles of association, each director has the full power to bind and represent the company in all aspects (e.g., entering into contracts on the company's behalf and representing it in dispute settlement). However, the articles of association or the board of directors' decision may limit the respective power and duties of each director. The board of directors has the authority to give a written power of attorney to one or more employees of the company or to some other persons for and on behalf of the company to perform specific legal actions if the board of directors cannot represent the company.

Laws Affecting M&A

[31]

- Indonesian Civil Code ('*ICC*').
- Law Number 40 of 2007 on PT ('*Law No. 40/2007*' *or* '*Company Law*').
- Law Number 25 of 2007 on Investment ('*Law No. 25/2007*').
- Law Number 9 of 2006 on Security Right over Warehouse Receipt as amended by Law Number 9 of 2011 ('*Law No. 9/2006*').
- Law Number 37 of 2004 on Bankruptcy and Suspension of Obligation for Payment of Debts ('*Law No. 37/2004*').
- Law Number 30 of 2004 as amended by Law Number 2 of 2014 on Notary Office ('*Law No. 30/2004*').

- Law Number 13 of 2003 on Manpower (‘*Law No. 13/2003*’).
- Law Number 42 of 1999 on Fiduciary Security (‘*Law No. 42/1999*’).
- Law Number 30 of 1999 on Arbitration and Alternative Dispute Resolution (‘*Law No. 30/1999*’).
- Law Number 5 of 1999 on Prohibition of Monopolistic Practice and Unfair Business Competition (‘*Law No. 5/1999*’).
- Law Number 4 of 1996 on Security Right over the Land (‘*Law No. 4/1996*’).
- Law Number 8 of 1995 on Capital Markets (‘*Law No. 8/1995*’).
- Law Number 7 of 1992 as further amended with Law Number 10 of 1998 on Banking (‘*Law No. 7/1992*’).
- Law Number 5 of 1960 on Agrarian (‘*Law No. 5/1960*’).
- Government Regulation Number 24 of 2018 on Electronic Single Submission System (‘*GR No. 24/2018*’).
- Government Regulation Number 57 of 2010 on Merger or Consolidation of Business Entities and the Acquisition of Shares of Companies Which May Cause Monopolistic Practices and Unfair Business Competition (‘*GR No. 57/2010*’).
- Government Regulation Number 131 of 2000 on Income Tax on Deposit and Saving Interest and Discounted of Bank Indonesia Certificate as lastly amended by Government Regulation Number 123 of 2015 on Amendment of Government Regulation Number 131 of 2000 on Income Tax on Deposit and Saving Interest and Discounted of Bank Indonesia Certificate (‘*GR No. 131/2000*’).
- Government Regulation Number 28 of 1999 on Merger, Consolidation, and Acquisition of Bank (‘*GR No. 28/1999*’).
- Government Regulation Number 27 of 1998 on Merger, Consolidation, and Acquisition of PT (‘*GR No. 27/1998*’).
- Government Regulation Number 24 of 1997 on Land Registration (‘*GR No. 24/1997*’).
- Presidential Regulation Number 44 of 2016 on Negative Investment List (‘*PR No. 44/2016*’).
- Minister of Trade Regulation Number 36/M-DAG/PER/9/ 2007 as lastly amended by Minister of Trade Regulation Number 07/M-DAG/PER/2/ 2017 on Trade Business License (‘*MoT Regulation No. 36/2007*’).
- OJK Regulation Number 9/POJK.04/2018 on Takeover of Public Companies (‘*OJK Regulation No. 9/POJK.04/2018*’).
- OJK Regulation Number 12/POJK.01/2017 on Implementation of Anti-Money Laundering and Terrorism-Financing Prevention Programs in the Financial Service Sector (‘*OJK Regulation No. 12/2017*’).
- OJK Regulation Number 74/POJK.04/2016 as lastly amended by OJK Regulation Number 58/POJK.04/2017 on Mergers or Consolidations of Public Company (‘*OJK Regulation No. 74/2016*’).
- OJK Regulation Number 2/POJK.04/2013 on Buy Back Shares Issued by the Issuer or Public Company in Market Condition Fluctuate Significantly (‘*OJK Regulation No. 2/2013*’).

Relevant Regulatory Authorities

[32]

(1) Ministry of Law and Human Rights (*'MOLHR'*)
In the event of merger and acquisition transactions, MOLHR is responsible for providing an approval on ratification of the company as a legal entity; approval on the amendment of articles of association of the company and the management of the company registry. In addition, the MOLHR will need to be notified of changes in the shareholding structure of any company.

(2) Indonesia Coordinating Investment Board (*'BKPM'*)
BKPM as the OSS Agency is responsible for providing regulations on investment in Indonesia; providing an approval relating to Investment such as Business License and Commercial or Operational Licenses for and on behalf of Ministries, Heads of Agencies, Governors, Regents and Mayors; conducting integrated one-stop service for providing license and non-license to the investor.

(3) Financial Service Authority (*'OJK'*)
OJK is responsible for providing regulations on financial services in Indonesia either for financial institutions or non-financial institutions as well as in the capital market sector, providing an approval for transactions in the financial service sector including merger and acquisition transactions.

(4) The Commission for the Supervision of Business Competition (*'Komisi Pengawas Persaingan Usaha'* or *'KPPU'*)
The KPPU is charged with the supervision of business competition pursuant to Law No. 5/1999. It is an independent commission, directly responsible to the President. Specifically, its tasks include:
   (a) Evaluate agreements that may result in monopoly practice or unfair business competition.
   (b) Evaluate business practice or the conducts of business actors that may result in monopoly or unfair business competition practices.
   (c) Evaluate whether or not a dominant position is abused that may result in monopoly or unfair business practices.
   (d) Take actions to address monopoly or unfair business practices, including receiving complaints, investigating, summoning business players, obtaining documents, and imposing administrative sanctions.
   (e) Issue recommendations and opinions on government policy in relation to government policies in relation to monopoly and unfair business practices.
   (f) Draft guidance and/or publications in relation to Law No. 5/1999.
   (g) Report the result of the Commission's work to the President and the People's Legislative Council (DPR).

(5) Industry-Specific Regulators

Depending on the business sector and the corporate action, notification or even approval from industry regulators may be necessary. As an example, the purchase of the shares of a bank that result in more than 40% of the shares being owned by one financial institution requires approval of OJK.

(6) Local Government (Provincial and/or Regency/City)
Local Government in the framework of investment in Indonesia has a role in providing an approval if delegated in accordance with its authority. Based on the implementation of regional autonomy, the local government may issue laws and regulations on matters including those relating to merger and acquisition transactions.

[33] It is possible for the investor to engage personally to submit the application to the OSS System or the Online SPIPISE from BKPM. Nonetheless, the investor may also delegate to other parties to handle this as long as there is a power of attorney. There is no differentiation in the timetable to obtain government approval either conducted by investor itself and/or through advisers, although advisors who specialize in certain approvals will be more familiar with the requirements and actual practices.

Controls/Restrictions on Foreign Investment

[34] Indonesia is open for foreign investment. The principle of Law No. 25/2007 is all business sectors are open to investment, both by foreign and domestic investors, unless they are closed or restricted by law. There are several sectors that are closed or otherwise restricted to foreign investment. Pursuant to Article 12 of Law No. 25/2007, business sectors that are closed for foreign investors are:

(a) Production of weapons, ammunition, explosive devices, and armaments.
(b) Business sectors that are explicitly declared to be closed by law.

Note that all foreign direct investment activities must be done through a PT, unless the investment through an alternative vehicle is permitted by law. We understand that in the following sectors, business activities conducted through a vehicle other than PT are possible:

(a) banking;
(b) construction services; and
(c) oil and gas exploration and exploitation.

[35] Company and foreign interest is denominated in terms of the percentage of the company's shares. The restrictions (e.g., maximum foreign shareholding and other conditions) on foreign investment in Indonesia are regulated under the Negative Investment List, which is set out under Annex I and II of PR No. 44/2016. Additionally, the following material restrictions are applicable pursuant to other laws and regulations:

- Insurance: maximum foreign ownership 80%, although a larger percentage can be held depending on the capital structure.
- Banking: maximum foreign ownership 99% but subject to certain restrictions on the number of shares that any one shareholder may hold.
- Finance companies: maximum foreign ownership 80%–85%.
- Nuclear and other energy power plant: maximum foreign ownership 95%.
- Transportation: maximum foreign ownership 49%–60%.

[36] A foreign investor may own (by acquisition of existing company or establishment of new one) 100% of shares in an Indonesian company unless it is restricted by law.

[37] As discussed above, the principle of Indonesia's investment policy is that all business sectors are open to investment unless it is closed or restricted (partially open) by the applicable law.[1] With the exception of few sectors all foreign investment activities must be conducted through a PT, formed in accordance with the provisions of Law No. 40/2007. Foreign investors' interest is denominated in terms of percentage of paid up capital in such PT(s) owned by that foreign investor. In turn, the maximum percentage of foreign shareholding in the restricted sectors must conform to the Negative Investment List (currently PR No. 44/2016).

[38] A domestic and foreign investment company is distinguished by whether or not a foreign person or entity owns any shares of a PT. If the answer is yes, the PT will be deemed to be a Foreign Investment Company ('*PT PMA*'). This classification does not factor in the percentage of the shares owned, with the consequence that share ownership by a foreign person or an entity in a PT, irrespective of how little, results in the PT being classified as PT PMA. Furthermore, the negative investment list does not discriminate between the acquisition of shares in an existing company and the creation of a new company. As such, any locally established SPV corporation whose shares are owned by a foreigner will be classified as PT PMA and thus subject to the Negative Investment List, irrespective of the foreign-owned percentage.

[39] Previously, as a matter of procedure to perfect the investors' rights, every corporate action that involves changes in the shareholding composition must be reported to and approved by both the MOLHR and BKPM. However, under GR No. 24/2018, with the new OSS system, business actors are not required to obtain any prior approval from the OSS agency, i.e., BKPM. This create a post-audit nature of the system, where audit by BKPM or the relevant ministries for compliance with regard to all corporate actions involving a company (e.g., establishment, change of shareholders of a company, change of capital structure of a company and/or conversion of a domestic investment company into a foreign investment company), fulfilment of Commitment and other monitoring/controlling will be conducted after such activity has been undertaken by the company.

[1] Certain business sectors are not open to investment (e.g., armaments) while others are restricted/ partially open based on the source of capital (domestic or foreign) and the scale of the business. Note that under the latest revision of the Negative Investment List the Government has introduced geographical-based restrictions.

[40] For those reasons, acquisition by way of purchasing the shares of the target company through a locally formed SPV raises a number of significant legal issues. First, the SPV will be classified as PT PMA, and it will be subject to the negative investment list itself. Second, even if the SPV serves merely as the holding company that will own the shares of the target company, the action will typically be done through sale and purchase of shares. Such corporate actions must be reported to, and in some cases get approval from, various regulators. Such actions typically require disclosure of the shareholding structure.

[41] Pursuant to Law No. 25/2007, foreign investment must assume the form of a PT. This entails the foreign investor subscribing to the company's shares, whether the foreign investor enters into the Indonesian market by way of establishing a new company or acquiring an existing one.

[42] The company (or target company) will be subject to and must comply with at least three regimes of formal approvals. The categories of permit regimes are:

(i) Approvals and corporate documents related to the company.
(ii) Approvals specific to foreign investment.
(iii) Approvals to conduct business operations.

Approvals and Corporate Documents Related to Incorporation

Establishment

[43] The procedure of incorporation is a two-staged process. First, the company incorporations (founding shareholders) enter into an agreement to incorporate, formalized by a notarial deed before a public notary. Second, the incorporators apply for the recognition from the Government to ratify the company incorporation.

Table of Incorporation Approvals and Corporate Documents

No	*Document Name*	*Issuing Authority*	*Time to Issue (As Regulated)*[2]	*Official Cost (IDR, 000)*
1	Legalization on the establishment of the company (*SK Pengesahan*)	Minister of Law and Human Rights (done by the notary)	Within a maximum period of Fourteen Days	IDR100 000 for check the company's name + IDR500 000 up to IDR1 000 000 for legalization on the establishment of the company as legal entity + IDR580 000 for Official Gazette of the Republic of Indonesia)
2	Business Identification Number (*Nomor Induk Berusaha*/ '*NIB*'). NIB is the first step towards getting the following licenses: (1) Certificate of Company Registration ('*Tanda Daftar Perusahaan*' or '*TDP*');	The OSS System.	Automatically issued after business owners has fulfilled the requirements.	No Cost

[2] Time to issue means the length of time after the required documents are submitted and deemed to be complete and correct. The issuance time does not take into account the verification process.

Table of Incorporation Approvals and Corporate Documents

No	*Document Name*	*Issuing Authority*	*Time to Issue (As Regulated)*[2]	*Official Cost (IDR, 000)*
	(2) Importer Identification Number ('*Angka Pengenal Impor*' or '*API*') if the business intends to import goods; (3) Customs Access ('*Akses Kepabeanan*') if the business intends to export and/or import goods.			
3	Trade Business License ('*SIUP*')	Minister of Trade (Delegated to BKPM through the OSS System)	Varies depending on the line of business	No Cost
4	Taxpayer Identification Number ('*NPWP*')	Director General of Tax (In the event that a company does not have an NPWP, OSS which was integrated with the	One Day	No Cost

Table of Incorporation Approvals and Corporate Documents

No	*Document Name*	*Issuing Authority*	*Time to Issue (As Regulated)*[2]	*Official Cost (IDR, 000)*
		system at the Directorate General of Taxes will process the NPWP.)		
5	Company Domicile Certificate (*SK Domisili*)	Local District Office (issued by PTSP)	Three Days	No Cost

[44] Under Law No. 40/2007, a company only attains its status as a legal entity, thus the separate liability and the capacity to take legal actions and own assets and bear liabilities on its own behalf, once the Minister of Law and Human Rights has recognized its existence. Recognition of existence is formalized when the Minister issues the Legalization on the establishment of the company (*SK Pengesahan Pendirian Badan Hukum Perseroan Terbatas*). To obtain the Legalization on the establishment of the company, the incorporator or its agent, must first reserve a name at the MOLHR to ensure that it has not been used by another Indonesian company, to avoid a rejection by the MOLHR of the company's deed of establishment and articles of association.

[45] In addition to the legalization on the establishment of the company, the company must also obtain a number of other documents in order for it to assume basic levels of operations. The list of approvals and documents related to incorporation are listed below.

Amendments to Articles of Association in the Event of Merger, Consolidation, Acquisition, and Separation

[46] Amendments to the company's articles of associations must be reported to or, in certain cases, get approval from the MOLHR. Such amendments are listed below:

No.	*Change to Articles of Association*	*Reporting*	*Approval*
1	Name and Domicile of the company	✓	✓
2	Purpose and business sector of the company	✓	✓
3	Duration of Establishment	✓	✓

No.	*Change to Articles of Association*	*Reporting*	*Approval*
4	Amount of Authorized Capital	✓	✓
5	Reduction of the Amount of Subscribed Capital	✓	✓
6	Reduction of the Paid-Up Capital	✓	✓
7	Change of Status from public to private company and vice versa	✓	✓
8	Change to current shareholders percentage that causes of change in control of the company (without changes to the amount of authorized, subscribed or paid up capital)	✓	✓
9	Changes to Articles of Association as part of Merger and Acquisition[3]	✓	✓
10	Changes of shareholder due to transfer of shares and/or change of number of shares owned (that does not cause change to control of company)	✓	✓
11	Other changes	✓	

[47] Law No. 40/2007 does not prescribe any penalty for failure to report. However, it is to be noted that the ownership of shares, and the rights attached thereto, only become perfect and enforceable against third parties upon letter of recognition or ratification by the Ministry.

Approvals Related to Foreign Investment

[48] Foreign investment in Indonesia may only be conducted through the form of a PT. Such companies will be termed PT PMA. In addition to the process of incorporation as set out in paragraphs **[43]**–**[47]**, the company must obtain investment-related licenses from BKPM. Generally, every PT PMA must obtain at least two licenses from BKPM. Nowadays, there are 2 (two) licenses that can be applied through the OSS System by business owners i.e., the Business License and the Commercial or Operational License.

[3] Acquisition is a specific legal concept under Law No. 40/2007, defined as the takeover of shares by a person or an entity that causes change in control of the company. Ordinary changes of shareholders need not approval from the Ministry but must be reported.

[49] Business Licenses are licenses issued by the OSS for and on behalf of Minister, Head of Agency, Governor, or Regent/Mayor after the business owners has completed the registration process and such license shall be used to commence operations and/or activities prior to the commencement of commercial operation by fulfilling the relevant requirements. Meanwhile, Commercial or Operational Licenses are licenses issued by the OSS for and on behalf of Minister, Head of Agency, Governor, or Regent/Mayor after the business owners has obtained the required Business License and commenced its commercial operation by fulfilling the relevant requirements.

[50] The GR No. 24/2018 outlines twenty sectors affected by business license reforms (as stated in Article 85 of GR No. 24/2018), including, but not limited to, energy and power, agriculture, forestry, public works and housing, fisheries, health, pharmaceutical and food, industry, communications and informatics, financial, tourism, education and culture, higher education, religious affairs, employment, police, cooperative, small and medium enterprises, and nuclear energy.

[51] The timeframe and costs associated with obtaining such licenses are listed below.

Table of Approvals Specific to Foreign Investment

No	*Document Name*	*Issuing Authority*	*Time to Issue (Days)*[4]	*Cost (IDR) (Official Cost)*
1	– Business Licenses – Commercial or Operational Licenses Business fields based on Article 85 GR No.24/ 2018	The OSS Agency (for and on behalf of Ministries, Heads of Agencies, Governors, Regents and Mayors)	Business license is issued after the commitment of location permit, environment permit/SPPL, building permit, SLF and any other business license prerequisites have been fulfilled and the payment (if required) has been completed. Operational/commercial license are issued automatically after the commitment statement is	

[4] Time to issue means the length of time after the required documents are submitted and deemed to be complete and correct.

Table of Approvals Specific to Foreign Investment

No	*Document Name*	*Issuing Authority*	*Time to Issue (Days)*[4]	*Cost (IDR) (Official Cost)*
			filed but shall take effect after the commitment has been fulfilled, including the relevant payment (if required).	
2	Licensing: – Licenses for Energy and Mineral Resources sector; – Licenses for Public Works and Housing sector; – Licenses for Financial sector; Business fields based on BKPM Regulation No.6/ 2018	BKPM on behalf of Sectoral Regulator through Online SPIPISE	Three days after the completion of required documents.	For Foreign Construction Services Agency is between USD5 000 and USD10 000. Meanwhile for other licenses there are no costs.
3	Investment Sector: – Licenses for a Foreign Company Representative Office (KPPA) for business other than construction and trade sectors;	BKPM on behalf of Sectoral Regulator through Online SPIPISE	– For Foreign Company Representative Office (KPPA) three days after the completion of the required documents; – For a branch opening three days after the completion of the required documents;	Varies based on sector

Table of Approvals Specific to Foreign Investment

No	*Document Name*	*Issuing Authority*	*Time to Issue (Days)*[4]	*Cost (IDR) (Official Cost)*
	– Licenses for a Branch Opening. For business owners whose business licenses are issued by Central PTSP; – Recommendation for a Limited Stay Visa (VITAS) for shareholders; – Recommendation for changing a Visit Stay Permit into Temporary Stay Permit (ITAS); – Recommendation for changing ITAS to Permanent Stay Permit (ITAP).		– For VITAS recommendation three days after the completion of the required documents; – For ITAS recommendation three days after the completion of the required documents; – For ITAP recommendation three days after the completion of the required documents.	

Table of Approvals Specific to Foreign Investment

No	*Document Name*	*Issuing Authority*	*Time to Issue (Days)*[4]	*Cost (IDR) (Official Cost)*
4	Custom and Tax Facilities – Facilities for machinery, capital goods and materials for investor in the industrial sector and the industrial sector that provide services; – Facilities for importing machinery and capital goods in the electric power sector; – Facilities for importing machinery and capital goods importation for contracts of work and Coal Contracts of Work; – Tax holiday; – Tax allowances	BKPM on behalf of Sectoral Regulator	For tax allowance is about eight days until twenty-three days depends on the documents completion and the result of trilateral meeting.	

[52] There are certain administrative charges involved when applying for certain approvals from the related government institutions (e.g., MOLHR, BKPM, etc.), notary, and lawyer where the amount will vary depending on the line of business.

[53] In running day-to-day business, the company may be managed by foreign or local directors except for the Personnel Director who must be an Indonesian national (*see* the Employment Considerations below for further elaboration). Furthermore, generally business lines in the form of PMA Companies are required to have a local partner.

[54] On a supervisory basis there are several government officials that will conduct supervision of the company:

- For a PT PMA and domestic investments ('*PT PMDN*') in Indonesia are administered and supervised by BKPM. Therefore, the relevant matters to merger and acquisition transactions must be reported to MOLHR and BKPM through the Online SPIPISE or the OSS System depending on the business field.
- OJK is responsible for supervising the takeovers, mergers or consolidations transactions involving public companies in Indonesia. In addition, OJK is responsible for ensuring compliance with the Capital Market Law, BAPEPAM & LK/OJK rules and the Indonesia Stock Exchange ('*IDX*') rules if the public company is listed on the IDX.
- The Business Competition Supervisory Commission (the '*Commission*' or '*KPPU*') has the authority to prohibit a range of restrictive agreements and abusive behaviours, including mergers and acquisitions that may result in monopolistic practices or unfair business competition.

[55] To conduct trade business in Indonesia every company either wholly owned by foreigner and/or jointly with domestic local partner or domestic company shall have trade business license pursuant to MoT Regulation No. 36/2007.

[56] The minimum capital requirement for foreign-owned company conducting trade business in Indonesia is currently more than IDR10 billion (USD719 000) pursuant to BKPM Regulation No. 6/2018.

[57] In conducting business in Indonesia, foreigner cannot own Right to Own land (*Hak Milik*). Instead, it is permitted to own subsidiary land rights. Indonesia's land law regime divides rights over land into a hierarchy of rights. A foreigner is permitted to own two specific land rights, which are Leasehold (Article 45 of Law No. 5/1960) and the Right to use (Article 41 of Law No. 5/1960). Furthermore, PT PMA may utilize three different types of land rights for their business activities, namely a Right to Cultivate, a Right to Build, or a Right to Use based on Article 22 of Law No. 25/2007 on Investments.

[58] Foreigners are permitted to own mining/mineral rights. For general mining, 100% foreign ownership is permitted. However, there is an obligation to divest 51% gradually over a period of five years after five years of commercial production. The timeline requires companies to divest at least 20% of their shares after six years, 30% after seven years, 37% after eight years, 44% after nine years and 51% after ten years.

Incentives for Foreign Investment

[59] Indonesia provides foreign investment with tax incentives. These incentives are regulated under Law No. 25/2007. Investment that is eligible for these facilities are investments with the following criteria:

(a) provides a substantial number of jobs;
(b) falls under the category of high priority investments;
(c) engaged in infrastructure construction;
(d) involve transfers technology;
(e) in a pioneer industry;
(f) located in a remote area, a less-developed area, a contiguous area or another area deemed to require development;
(g) is environmentally sustainable;
(h) involves research, development, and innovative activities;
(i) is engaged in partnership with micro, small, and medium enterprises or cooperatives; or
(j) in an industry that uses domestically produced capital goods or machinery or equipment.

[60] Additionally, pursuant to BKPM Regulation No. 6/2018, there are investment incentives for foreign investors such as facilities of:

- Facilities for machinery, capital goods and materials for investors in the industrial sector and the industrial sector that provides services.
- Facilities for importing machinery and capital goods in the electric power sector.
- Facilities for importing machinery and capital goods importation for contracts of work and coal contracts of work.
- Tax holiday; and
- Tax allowances.

Free trade areas and free ports in Indonesia are located in Batam, Bintan, and Karimun, goods entering into and goods delivered between free trade areas are exempted from import duty and excise. In addition, no import taxes including value added tax, local service tax and income tax are collected on these goods. Goods that originate from a free trade area that enter into the Indonesian customs area are liable to import duties and taxes. Free ports are areas that are separate from the customs area and as a result free from the imposition of customs duties, value added tax, and tax on luxury goods and customs. Furthermore, in order to accelerate the economic development and job growth, the government enacted Law Number 39 of 2009 on Special Economic Zones ('*Kawasan Ekonomi Khusus*' or '*KEK*') that defines zones with certain boundaries within the territories of the Unitary State of the Republic of Indonesia, also designated to carry out the economic function and are granted certain facilities and incentives.

Government Guarantee Against Expropriation or Nationalization

[61] Under Law No. 25/2007, the government of Republic of Indonesia will neither nationalize nor take over the ownership right of any investor, unless 'by primary legislation' (*undang-undang*). This could be interpreted as expropriation by the operation of existing primary legislation or that the government will enact a new legislation each time an expropriation is to take place. Furthermore, there is no explicit guarantee that the Government will not expropriate or nationalize other than this provision.

[62] However, if the government of Republic of Indonesia conducts nationalization, it will provide fair compensation as determined by market price. Market price is to be determined based on international practices, to be set by independent appraisers appointed by the Government and the investor(s). It is of note that the law does not explicitly provide for calculation method, in particular whether or not the compensation price is based on the current market price of the expropriated asset or takes into account future price.

[63] If there is no consent between the parties concerning on compensation or indemnity, the settlement may be conducted through arbitration process. Furthermore, according to bilateral investment treaties entered into by the Republic of Indonesia and other states, expropriation or nationalization may take place under the following conditions:

(a) The measures are taken for a lawful purpose or public purpose and under the process of law.
(b) The measures are non-discriminatory.
(c) The measures are accompanied by provision for the payment of prompt, adequate and effective compensation and shall amount to the fair market value without delay before the measure of dispossession becomes acknowledged. Such market value shall be determined in accordance with internationally acknowledged practices or methods. In the event such fair market value cannot be determined, it shall be such reasonable amount as may be mutually agreed between the Parties and it shall be freely transferable in freely usable currencies from the party.

Profit Repatriation and Payment of Dividends Abroad

[64] Law No. 25/2007 provides investors the right to transfer and repatriate in foreign currency, among others, capital, profits, bank interests, dividends, and other income, as well as funds necessary to purchase raw materials and capital goods. Furthermore, the bilateral investment treaties also guarantee the payment of principal and interest on foreign loans or payment relating to the investment, in which such investment including Intellectual Property Rights ('*IPR*') and technical process. However, the provision regarding the right to transfer and repatriate in foreign currency does not apply to transactions conducted by PT PMA to other companies (other than the investor[5]) in respect to Law Number 7 of 2011 on Currency for Foreign Investment in Indonesia *jo.* Bank Indonesia Regulation No. 17/3/PBI/2015 on the Mandatory Use of the Rupiah in Indonesia.

[65] Such transfers are subject to the applicable law and thus the procedure to effectuate these transfers must conform to the procedure set out under the law. In addition, these transfers do not prejudice the government's rights to:

- Require the investor to report such transfers.
- Impose taxes, royalties, and/or other government revenue pursuant to applicable law.
- Protection of creditors' rights pursuant to the applicable law.
- Implementation of the law to avoid state losses.

[66] Finally, one should note that the Minister of Finance or state investigator (the police, the Attorney General Office, and other civil service charged with investigation) may request a bank to withhold the transfer pending the fulfilment of the investor's obligations to the state. Equally, the court may impose a hold on a transfer and order the bank to withhold the transfer based on a lawsuit made against the investor. Banks and other institutions that receive such court order must comply.

Financing

[67] The financing for acquisition may be conducted through loan and/or syndicated loan, depending on the size of the transaction. Furthermore, the reasons to use syndicated loan are to spread out the risk of the transaction and to avoid the Legal Lending Limit, because the characteristics of syndicated loans among one or more creditors/lending institutions allow for a larger loan amount and longer loan period.

[68] Pursuant to Bank Indonesia Regulation No. 7/3/PBI/2005 as amended by Bank Indonesia Regulation No. 8/13/2006 on the Legal Lending Limit for Commercial Banks, domestic banks may undertake lending to other parties. The requirements of lending are as follows:

(a) The provision of funds to borrower associated with a bank is set at the maximum amount of 10% of bank capital.
(b) The provision of funds to borrower not associated with a bank is set at the maximum amount of 20% of bank capital.
(c) The provision of funds to group of borrowers not associated with a bank is set at the maximum amount of 25% of bank capital.

[69] However, pursuant to Bank Indonesia Regulation No. 18/19/PBI/2016 on Foreign Exchange Transactions Against Rupiah between Banks and Foreign Parties,

5 'Investor' means an individual or a business entity that makes an investment, who may be a domestic investor and a foreign investor.

Banks are prohibited from performing transactions with Foreign Parties,[6] among others on:

(a) Lending or financing in Rupiah and/or foreign currencies, except for:
   (1) Non-cash credit or financing or guarantee related to investment activities in Indonesia obtaining counter guaranty from a Prime Bank or the availability of security deposit of 100% from the value of guarantee's given.
   (2) Credit or financing in the form of syndicates.
   (3) Credit Cards.
   (4) Consumption credit or financing used in the country.
   (5) Intraday overdrafts in Rupiah and foreign currencies supported by authenticated documents showing confirmation on the inflow of funds to the concerned account on the same day.
   (6) Overdrafts in Rupiah and foreign currencies for administrative costs.
   (7) Takeover of bills from the government appointed body that has to manage the concerned Bank assets in the context of restructuring Indonesia's banking by Foreign Parties whose payments guaranteed by Prime Banks.
(b) Placements in Rupiah.
(c) Purchase of Securities in Rupiah issued by Foreign Parties, excluding:
   (1) Purchase of Securities related to activities of goods export from Indonesia and goods import to Indonesia as well as domestic trades.
   (2) Purchase of bank drafts in Rupiah issued by banks overseas for the interest of Indonesian Workers (*TKI*).
(d) Interoffice billings in Rupiah.
(e) Interoffice billings in foreign currencies in the context of Lending or Financing in foreign countries.
(f) Capital investments in Rupiah.
(g) Foreign Exchange Transactions against Rupiah if the transactions or potential transactions are related to structured products.

These exclusions also apply for relevant transactions based on shariah principle. Therefore, it can be concluded that domestic bank may undertake lending for large scale-investment as long as the lending is in accordance with Bank Indonesia Regulation on Legal Lending Limit for Commercial Banks and Foreign Exchange Transactions Against Rupiah Between Banks and Foreign Parties.

[70] Pursuant to Law No. 4/1996 on Security Right over the Land (*Hak Tanggungan*), type of assets that can be encumbered by security right over the land are immovable assets (land) and structures attached to the land and the holder of security right over the land shall be individual or a legal entity, which divided into: (a) Indonesia citizen; (b) Foreign citizen (domiciled or not domiciled in Indonesia); (c)

[6] Foreign Parties are (a) Foreign Citizen; (b) Foreign legal entity or other foreign institution; (c) Indonesian citizen having permanent resident status of other state and not domiciled in Indonesia; (d) Bank office in offshore which is headquartered in Indonesia; (e) the representative office from a company incorporated in Indonesia.

Indonesia legal entity; (d) Foreign legal entity (having representatives office in Indonesia or headquartered in overseas).[7] Therefore, it is permissible for a foreign lender to take security over local immovable property in Indonesia.

[71] Indonesia has no foreign exchange controls and funds may be transferred to and from abroad. However, transfer exceeding USD10 000 must be reported to the Bank Indonesia. The control over the transfer of funds to foreign lender may be in the form of Foreign Exchange Flow Report (*Lalu Lintas Devisa*) according to Bank Indonesia Regulation No. 16/22/PBI/2014 on Reporting of Foreign Exchange Flows and Activity Reporting of Implementation on Prudential Principles in Offshore Loans Management by Non-Bank Corporations. The Foreign Exchange Flow Report may contain: (a) Trading transaction of goods and services, other transactions between Indonesia citizen and foreigners; (b) the mutation of foreign financial assets and/or foreign financial obligation; (c) plan and/or realization of offshore debt. This Foreign Exchange Flow Report shall be submitted to Bank Indonesia, unless stipulated otherwise by prevailing laws and regulations and if the parties do not submit the Foreign Exchange Flow Report, shall be imposed by administrative sanctions.

[72] Pursuant to Article 1 of GR No. 131/2000 as lastly amended by GR No. 123 of 2015 on Income Tax for Deposit and Saving Interest and Discounted of Bank Indonesia Certificate, interest derived from deposit or saving placed in offshore through the bank incorporated in Indonesia or branches of foreign bank in Indonesia subjected to final income tax. Therefore, it is permissible for local/domestic companies to hold offshore bank accounts. Besides that, pursuant to Article 21 of Law Number 7 of 2011 on Currency for Foreign Investment in Indonesia, the currency of Indonesia, Rupiah shall be used for every transaction relating to the payment of transaction and/or other financial transactions located in Indonesia. However, the obligation to use Rupiah can be avoided for certain transactions, among others: in the event of the implementation of the State Revenues and Expenditures Budget (*APBN*), acceptance or distribution of grants from/to offshore, international trade transaction, savings in bank in the form of foreign currency and international payment transaction.

Mergers under Law No. 40/2007 on PT

Shareholder Rights in Acquisition

[73] Acquisition under Indonesian Law is a specific legal concept, distinct from ordinary purchase or transfer of shares. Law No. 40/2007 defines Acquisition as the legal conduct undertaken by a legal entity or a person for the purpose of obtaining shares of a company that results in the change in the control over the target company. Shareholders of the target company have the following rights in respects of an Acquisition.

[7] Frieda Husni Hasbullah, *Hukum Kebendaan Perdata Jilid 2*, Jakarta, Ind-Hill Co, 2002.

Quorum and Approval to Pass Acquisition Resolution

[74] Acquisition under Law No. 40/2007 takes place by way of issuance of new shares (initiated by target company board of directors) or by way of acquisition of existing shares (initiated by the shareholders). Both routes towards acquisition must be approved by a GMS resolution.

[75] GMS approval for the purpose of acquisition for both routes is governed under Articles 87 and 89 of Law No. 40/2007. For the purpose of acquisition GMS quorum is formed if voting shares are present or represented. In turn, resolution of approval is deemed to have passed if the voting shares present approve. Note that each PT's articles of association may set a higher threshold for quorum and vote to pass the resolution.

[76] The GMS must be held in the company domicile or in the place where the company does its main business and in the event the company is public company, the GMS is to be held in the domicile of the stock exchange where the company shares are listed and must be located in the territory of Republic of Indonesia. Apart from those provisions, the GMS may also be held via teleconference, video conference or other vehicles for electronic media.

Right of First Refusal

[77] In the event of sale of existing shares by current shareholders, where the articles of association stipulates, the selling shareholders must first offer such shares to the existing shareholders. The offeree shareholders have the right to subscribe to the offered shares in proportion to percentage of shares they currently own. The offer will be valid for thirty days since it is made and the selling shareholders may not withdraw the offer during this period. Only where the thirty-day period has lapsed can the selling shareholders offer the shares to third parties. In the event of new shares issuance, the company must offer the new shares to existing shareholders in the same proportion as they own (*see* Articles 43, 57 and 58 of Law No. 40/2007).

[78] The right of refusal remains applicable even if the GMS, the board of directors and the board of commissioners have approved the acquisition. As a consequence, it is theoretically possible for existing shareholders to block an acquisition by invoking their rights to first refusal. To circumvent the uncertainty, the existing shareholders would decide amongst themselves the percentage of the shares they would take up. To lock the shareholders, the potential acquirer would subsequently enter into agreement with each of the shareholders to waive their rights to subscribe to the shares.

Approval by Company Organs

[79] The articles of association may also stipulate that the Company organs (GMS, board of directors and/or board of commissioners) must approve transfer any form of share transfer.

Conformity to Shareholder Criteria

[80] The articles of association may list the criteria that a prospective shareholder must meet in order to own and exercise his rights over the shares. The criteria for owning the shares must be in accordance with the applicable law. Shareholders who do not meet these criteria may own the shares but cannot exercise their rights to the shares, such as receiving dividends or voting.

Share Buyback

[81] Shareholders who disagree to the acquisition may request the PT to purchase their shares at 'reasonable price' under a buyback mechanism, but subject to the restrictions discussed.

Directors' Duties

Directors Duties in Merger and Consolidation (Penggabungan dan Peleburan)

[82] Merger and Consolidation are two specific legal concepts under Law No. 40/2007. Merger is defined as the legal act whereby a company merges with another existing company such that the assets and liabilities of the merging company transfers to the company that receives them, and the merging company ceases to exist by law.

[83] Consolidation is an action conducted by two or more companies by way of establishing a new company, which by law receives the assets and liabilities of the consolidating companies and the consolidating companies cease to exist by law.

[84] In the event of merger, the board of directors shall draw up draft of merger and submitted that draft to the GMS of each company to obtain its approval, after obtaining the approval of the board of commissioners of each company. Meanwhile, certain companies in merger may need approval from the relevant government agencies in accordance with prevailing laws and regulation in the event of conducting merger. Furthermore, in the event of acquisition, before performing the legal action of acquisition, the board of directors shall have approval from the GMS. The board of directors of the company shall draw up draft of acquisition and obtain approval from board of commissioners.

[85] Furthermore, the board of directors of the company which will perform the merger, consolidation, acquisition, and segregation are also obliged to publish the abstract of the draft of merger, consolidation, acquisition or segregation in at least one newspaper and publish it in writing to the employees of the company that will perform the merger, consolidation, acquisition or segregation no later than thirty days before the invitation of the GMS.

Directors Duties in Acquisition (Pengambilalihan)

[86] Acquisition is a specific legal concept under Law No. 40/2007, defined as the *'legal act conducted by a person or a legal entity for the takeover of the shares of the (target)* *company that results in the change of control of such company.'*[8] This concept is thus distinguished from ordinary share purchase that does not alter the control over the target company.

[87] Law No. 40/2007 does not explicitly define what constitutes control. The test for control is set out under sectoral regulations for companies whose business fall under the regulations' scope (e.g., capital market regulations for publicly listed companies, and banking and insurance for banks and insurance business, respectively). For other companies to whom sectoral regulations do not apply, control is defined as a shareholder(s)' capacity to:

(a) Appoint and dismiss members of the board of directors or board of commissioners.
(b) Pass resolution to amend the company's articles of association.

[88] Furthermore, takeover under Law No. 40/2007 may take place by way of having the target company directors issuing new shares for the acquirer to subscribe to and pay up or by direct purchase from the existing shareholders. Furthermore, Law No. 40/2007 provides that takeover may be BOD-driven (by way of the BOD issuing new shares for the acquirer to subscribe to and pay up) or shareholder-driven (sale of existing shares between the existing shareholders and the acquirer).

Issues Concerning Hostile Acquisition

[89] Law No. 40/2007 does not specifically regulate for situations where the target company's BOD resists the takeover.

Form of Consideration

[90] In general, shares will be paid up in the form of money but there is possibility that shares will be paid up in some other form. The paying up of shares in some other form apart from money must be accompanied by giving the value or the price, type or kind, status, domicile as considered necessary for the sake of clarity regarding such paying up:

- The paid up of such shares is required to valuation process in accordance with market prices and if no market value available, the reasonable value will be specified based on appraisal techniques most suitable to the characteristics of the payment based on the best relevant information by an expert which is not affiliated with the company. The paid up of shares in the form of immovable assets shall be announced in one or more newspapers within period of fourteen days after the signing of the deed of establishment or after the GMS resolves on such paying up of shares and according to Law No. 40/2007 there is no restriction on disposal of shares acquired as a result of shares that paid up in some other form instead of money.

[8] *See* Art. 1 para. (11) and Art. 125 para. (3) Law No. 40/2007.

Financial Assistance

[91] In general, there is no specific requirement whether the company can provide corporate guarantee. This guarantee used by a reason of the guarantor has equal economic interest in the business with the borrower at least in the following circumstances:

- The guarantor as a director and the majority shareholders of the company, personally participate to guarantee company's debt.
- The parent company guarantees the debt of its subsidiaries.

[92] The company's articles of association needs to be examined to see whether the provision therein bars the guarantor company from making such guarantee. Where no such provision exists, the purpose and the objective of the company needs to be examined to see whether the guarantee is in line with such purpose and objective. Specifically, for public company pursuant to BAPEPAM Letter No. S-1505/PM/1997, for the protection of public shareholders, if the company acts as a corporate guarantor for its subsidiaries, the company shall have 99.9% shares from the total amount of paid up shares in its subsidiaries.

[93] The company may obtain financial assistance for buying its own shares as long as it does not contradict with Bank Indonesia Regulation No. 7/3/PBI/2005 as amended by Bank Indonesia Regulation No. 8/13/2006 on the Legal Lending Limit for Commercial Banks for loans from domestic bank. However, from lending such loans, pursuant to OJK Regulation No. 12/POJK.01/2017, the financial service sector shall apply customer due diligence and enhanced due diligence[9] to the debtor in order to know the identity of the debtor, to monitor customer transaction including the reporting of suspicious transactions. Thus, proof of solvency is not required since the bank applies such principles.

Security Interests

[94] Under Indonesian Law, there two types of securities. The first security is a guarantee; the guarantee can be conducted by an individual or a corporate. The other security is security over assets which divided into four types such as: (a) pledge; (b) fiduciary security; (c) security right over the land; (d) security right over warehouse receipt.

[95] There is a requirement to register security in Indonesia, even though not all guarantees must be registered. The securities that must be registered are as follows:

(a) Fiduciary security, by signing a notarial deed by a notary in Indonesian and registration by online mechanism according to Directorate General of Public

[9] Customer Due Diligence (CDD) is an activity such as identification, verification and monitoring conducted by Bank to ensure that transaction is in line with profile of Customer and Enhanced Due Diligence is a more comprehensive CDD conducted by Bank at the time of dealing with the high-risk Customer including Politically Exposed Person of the possibility of money laundering and financing of terrorism.

Administration Circular Letter No. AHU-06.OT.03.01/2013 *Jo.* Article 14 paragraph (1) and Article 16 paragraph (2) of Law No. 42/1999. As an evidence of registration, the applicant will get registration statement, which can be downloaded in the website. The type of assets of this security is movable (intangible or tangible) assets and immovable assets, especially building that cannot be encumbered with Security Rights over land referred to in Law No. 4/1996 on Security Right over the Land (*Hak Tanggungan*) which remain in control of the giver of the fiduciary, as collateral for the repayment of certain debt, which gives priority to the receiver's debt against other creditors.

(b) Security Rights over land: by signing a *hak tanggungan* deed before a Land Deed Official (*Pejabat Pembuat Akta Tanah*) and registering such deed at the Land Office. Upon such registration at *the hak tanggungan land book*, *hak tanggungan* will be perfected. A certificate is an evidence of registration.

(c) Security right over warehouse receipt: by signing a deed of security agreement, notifying the Registration Centre (PT Kliring Berjangka Indonesia) and the warehouse manager, annotating at the Registry Book of Security, and obtaining a confirmation of the notification.

[96] In the event of insolvency, pursuant to Article 1134 ICC, pledge and mortgage are superior to privilege, unless stipulated otherwise by the law. In Article 95 paragraph (4) Law No. 13/2003 on Manpower stated that in the event of bankruptcy or liquidation as referred to prevailing laws, employees have rights to precedent payment. This priority based on Article 138 of Law No. 37/2004 on Bankruptcy and Suspension of Obligation for Payment of Debts. In addition, on 12 September 2014, the Constitutional Court of the Republic of Indonesia (Constitutional Court) issued Decision No. 67/PUU-XI/2013 states that:

> *The payment of unpaid salaries of worker/labor is ahead of all types of creditors, including on secured creditor's claim, claim of the state's right, auction office, and public bodies which are established by the Government, while the payment of other rights of worker/labor shall take precedence over all claims, including claim of the state's right, auction office, and public bodies which are established by the Government, except for secured creditor's claim.*

[97] Furthermore, the suspect period is defined as the period which runs from the date on which the debtor ceases payments. Any transactions undertaken by the debtor in this period may be declared void. If they were undertaken against payment, proof would be needed that the persons entering into a contract with the debtor were aware that the latter had ceased payments. In Indonesia, pursuant to Law No. 37/2004 distinguish between insolvency and bankruptcy. Insolvency occurs if a company following its bankruptcy declaration by the court: (i) no composition plan is submitted by the company to the creditors, (ii) a composition plan is submitted but subsequently rejected by the creditors, or (iii) a composition plan is submitted and subsequently approved by the creditors but is not ratified by the court. Meanwhile, for bankruptcy, a company's bankruptcy proceedings are pronounced by the court if it fulfils the following test: (i) the company has at least two creditors (plurality of creditors); and (ii) at least one of the two debts is currently due and payable. Therefore, after the company declared bankrupt by the court, the debtor cannot conduct any transaction for the company. Nevertheless, before the declaration of bankruptcy every creditor, public prosecutor, bank Indonesia, OJK may submit application to the court to (i) determine security seizure on all or any part of debtor's assets or (ii) appoint the temporary receiver to control the management of debtor's business and payment to the creditor. This application may be granted, if intended to protect the interest of the creditor.

Completion Formalities

[98] The formalities that required in order conducting transfer of shares, land or other assets among others:

(a) For transfer of shares in merger and acquisition transaction, rights over shares shall be transferred with a deed of transfer of rights. Then, the deed of transfer of rights or its copy shall be submitted to the company in writing and the board of directors shall record the transfer of rights over shares in the register of shareholders/special register and announce the amendment on the structure of shareholders to the *MOLHR* at least thirty days since the registration of the transfer of rights to be registered in the Company Registry.

(b) For transfer of land, pursuant to GR No. 24/1997 *jo.* Law No. 5/1960, transfer of land may be conducted by means: sale-purchase, lease, grant, and inclusion in the company, auction, testamentary succession and consolidation of merger of the company. The requirements that are needed for such transactions include such as deed of transfer made by Land Deed Official (*Pejabat Pembuat Akta Tanah* or PPAT); then the deed of transfer shall be listed in Land Book in Land Registry Office, after which the certificate of ownership of land will be issued by the Land Registry Office.

[99] In Indonesia, the most important thing is the method of transfer (*levering*). This transfer is divided into two forms, transfer of movable asset, which in turn is divided into transfer of tangible movable asset and transfer of intangible movable asset, and transfer of immovable asset. The transfer of intangible movable asset conducted from hand to hand, means that factual transfer and juridical transfer are conducted simultaneously. Meanwhile, for transfer of immovable asset, factual transfer and juridical transfer are conducted at different times. This transfer is not only conducted through factual transfer but shall be made transfer letter (*akte van transport*) or shall be registered.

Costs and Fees

[100] The main costs and fees that will arise in relations to merger and acquisition are notary fees; obtaining a decision on the approval for amendments to the articles of association; an announcement required by Law No. 40/2007; and related government fees and tax.

[101] Generally, no government fee will be charged for processing government approval for merger and acquisition.

[102] According to Law No. 40/2007, before conducting merger the board of directors shall draft brief plan of merger which comprises:

(a) The name and domicile of each company in the merger.
(b) The reasons and explanations of the board of directors of the company in the merger and the merger requirements.
(c) Procedures of valuation and conversion of shares in the merging company into shares of the surviving company.
(d) The draft for any amendment of the articles of association of the surviving company.
(e) The financial report which covering the last three financial years from each of the company in the merger.
(f) The plans for continuing or terminating the business activities of the company in the merger.
(g) A pro forma balance sheet of the surviving company in accordance with accounting principles generally applied in Indonesia.
(h) Method of settlement of the status, rights and obligations of the members of the board of directors, board of commissioners and employees of the merging company.
(i) Method of settlement of the rights and obligations of the merging company against third party.
(j) Method of settlement of the rights of shareholders who do not agree to the merger of the company.
(k) Names of the members of the members of the board of directors and board of commissioners and the wages, honoraria, and allowances for members of the board of directors and board of commissioners of the surviving company.
(l) Estimated period for implementation of the merger.
(m) Report on the circumstances, development and result achieved of each of the company in the merger.
(n) Main activities of each company in the merger and changes which occurred in the current financial year.
(o) Details of problems arising during the current financial year which affected the activities of the company in the merger.

[103] That brief plan must be published in at least one newspaper and announce it in writing to the employees of the company which planning to conduct merger, the brief plan must be drawn up in a deed of merger before a notary in Bahasa Indonesia and also shall be attached with the application to obtain approval of the MOLHR and the delivery notification to the MOLHR of the amendment of the articles of association.

[104] There are disclosure requirements, pursuant to Article 127 paragraph (2) of the Company Law, the board of directors of the company that is to enter into an acquisition must make an announcement of the brief plan to the public through at least one newspaper. The brief plan of the acquisition must include at least:

(a) Name and domicile of the acquiring company and the company to be acquired.
(b) The reasons and explanations of the board of directors of the acquiring company and company to be acquired.
(c) The financial reports for the most recent financial year of the acquiring company and the company to be acquired.
(d) Procedures for valuation and conversion of shares of the company to be acquired into exchange shares if payment for the acquisition is to be made by shares.
(e) The number of shares to be acquired.
(f) Preparation of funding.
(g) Pro forma consolidated balance sheet of the acquiring company after the acquisition compiled in accordance with accounting principles generally applied in Indonesia.
(h) Method of settlement of rights of shareholders who do not agree the acquisition.
(i) Method of settlement of the status, rights and obligations of members of the board of directors, board of commissioners, and employees of the company to be acquired.
(j) Estimate of the period of implementation of the acquisition, including the period for granting a power of attorney from the shareholders to the company's board of directors to assign shares.
(k) Draft of any amendment of the articles of association of the company resulting from the acquisition.

[105] If an acquisition of shares is conducted directly by the shareholders, the above details summary shall not apply. However, upon the completion of the acquisition, the board of directors is required to disclose the acquisition by announcing it a newspaper not later than thirty days as of the effective date of the acquisition.

[106] If the merger and acquisition involves PT PMA or PT PMDN, a report must be submitted to the OSS System or SPIPISE BKPM for the relevant Sectoral Ministries, Agencies and/or Regional Government to monitor/supervise in accordance with the applicable relevant laws and regulations.

[107] Disclosure is also required to be made to KPPU for acquisition which results in total assets of IDR2.5 trillion or total revenue of IDR5 trillion. If the two or more parties involved in the acquisition are companies engaging in the business of banking, the disclosure is required if the acquisition results in total assets of more than IDR20 trillion.

[108] For public company acquisition, both parties shall consider the percentage of the shares, since according to OJK Regulation No. 11/POJK.04/2017 on Reporting of Substantial Shareholdings in Public Company regulates the obligation to report substantial shareholdings and any change of 0.5% or more of the shareholdings by anyone who directly or indirectly holds 5% or more of the total issued shares in a public company. Explicitly said, the ultimate beneficial owners are now required to report their shareholding.

Dividends

[109] The only source of dividend that Law No. 40/2007 recognizes is distributable profit. Company profits may be distributed as dividends only if these conditions are met:

- The company books net profits in the financial year.
- The net profit in that financial year amounts to more than the cumulative losses sustained in the previous years.
- The company has a reserve amounting to at least 20% of its subscribed and paid up capital.
- The GMS does not pass a resolution to allocate or expend the profits in a different manner.

[110] Law No. 40/2007 does not discriminate between foreign or domestic shareholders. Shares entitle its owners to, among others, receive dividends, and this right is contingent upon ownership of such shares, not the nationality of the owners. That said, Law No. 25/2007 sets out procedural restrictions on profits or dividends repatriation, such as taxation, compliance with applicable law, and settlement of outstanding obligations.

[111] With respect to taxation, the difference between domestic shareholders and foreign shareholders are as follows:

- Dividends for resident recipients are subject to Article 23 of Law No. 7/1983 on Income Tax, as already amended by Law No. 7/1991, Law No. 10/1994, Law No. 17/2000, and Law No. 36/2008 ('*Income Tax Law*'), withholding at 15%. The amount withheld constitutes a prepayment of the corporate tax liability for the company earning the dividends.
- Dividends for non-resident recipients are 20% (lower for treaty countries) final withholding tax is due on dividends paid to a non-resident recipient.

[112] With respect to reserves, Law No. 40/2007 recognizes two kinds of reserves: Mandatory Reserve and Other Reserves. Mandatory Reserve is intended to cover possibility of future losses. Its use is restricted to cover losses that other reserves cannot cover.

[113] Generally every company must set aside money from net profits (profit after tax) towards setting up and maintaining a Mandatory Reserve. The amount of the Mandatory Reserve is 20% of the paid-up capital. The obligation to form and set up such Mandatory Reserve arises only where the company books net profit that covers the losses sustained in the previous year. Note, however, that dividends may not be paid out to the shareholders until both previous years' losses have been covered and the 20% Mandatory Reserve is met.

[114] Mandatory Reserve needs not be in cash, however it must be sufficiently liquid and cannot be distributed as dividends.

Purchase of Own Shares

[115] Pursuant to Article 37 of Law No. 40/2007, repurchase of shares of company must not cause reductions in capital unless the shares are withdrawn. In the event of repurchase of shares by the company and any pledge of shares or fiduciary security over shares held by the company itself or by some other company whose shares are directly or indirectly owned by the company does not exceed 10% of the total amount of capital subscribed in the company unless otherwise provided legislative regulation in capital market sector. Then, the bought back shares may be held by the company for not more than three years, these restrictions are intended so that the company may determine whether the shares will be sold or withdrawn by means of a reduction in capital. In order to be able to conduct a buyback of shares it is necessary to consider the equilibrium repurchase price (ERP) of the bought back shares.

The Corporate Veil

[116] There are two ways a parent company can become liable for the debts or other liabilities of its subsidiaries under Indonesian Law. First, by guaranteeing the obligations of the subsidiary and, second, if it meets one of the criteria listed under Article 3 paragraph (2) of Law No. 40/2007.

[117] A parent's guarantee may set aside the corporate veil and may render the parent company liable for the liabilities of its subsidiary's obligations. Guarantee under Indonesian Law is an agreement, made for the benefit of the oblige, under which a third party binds itself to fulfil the obligations of an obligor where such obligor fails to fulfil the obligations themselves. The law makes no distinction between whether the guarantor is a parent company or a natural person shareholder or an independent third person.

[118] With respect to Article 3 paragraph (2) of Law No. 40/2007, the law provides that the parent company may become personally liable if one of these criteria is met:

(a) The requirements for the company as a legal entity has not or is no longer fulfilled.
(b) The relevant shareholder directly or indirectly and in bad faith exploits the company for his personal interests.
(c) The relevant shareholder is involved in an act against the law committed by the company.
(d) The relevant shareholder directly or indirectly and in contravention of the law utilizes the company's assets, which results in the assets of the company becoming insufficient to fulfil the company's debts.

[119] Another significant issue concerning lifting the corporate veil is the individual directors' and commissioners' liabilities. In the event of bankruptcy caused by the board of commissioners' fault or negligence in supervising the board of directors in managing the company and the company's assets are insufficient to pay all of the company's liabilities, every member of the board of directors and the board of commissioners are personally and jointly and severally liable to settle the company's outstanding debts.

Insolvency

[120] The main implications of buying shares or business which have gone into insolvency is, if after buying shares, the investor become majority shareholder then the investor shall manage the interest of all creditors as well as all debts of the company. Before, the investor buys shares of the targeted company which has gone to insolvency, it is necessary to consider the interests of the minority shareholders of the company, the company's employee, creditors, and other business partners of the company as well as the public and fair business competition.

[121] On buying shares or business that has gone into insolvency, there are special considerations that may arise in relation to the status of the company, whether the PT will be dissolved or will still continue its business.

Dissolution of a Bankrupt Company

[122] After being declared as bankrupt, a company is not automatically dissolved. The dissolution of a company after the bankruptcy process complete depends on the Judge Decision on the request of such dissolution. Pursuant to Article 142 of the Company Law, there are two reasons of company dissolution which are related to bankruptcy, namely:

(a) By the revocation of bankruptcy pursuant to Commercial Court Decision which has a binding legal force, the bankruptcy assets are not enough to pay the bankruptcy cost.
(b) Because the bankruptcy assets of a company which has been declared bankrupt is in a state of insolvency as provided in the Bankruptcy and Postponement of Debt Settlement Obligation Law.

[123] Furthermore, Article 18 paragraph (1) of Law No. 37/2004 provides that if a company is bankrupt so that it cannot afford to pay its debt, the creditor may request an application of the company dissolution to the Supervising Judge on the Decision of the bankruptcy statement submitted by the Debtor. Based on such creditor request, the Supervising Judge will propose to the Commercial Court, and after validly summon or hearing the Debtor, the Supervising Judge may decide to revoke the decision of bankruptcy statement. Based on such Commercial Court Decision, a company may be dissolved. The dissolution of a company is followed with a settlement so that the creditor will be entitled to obtain repayment from such settlement.

The Company Still Continues Its Business

[124] Not every company that has been through a bankruptcy process will be dissolved. Pursuant to the elucidation of Law No. 37/2004, there is a Business Continuity Principle in Law No. 37/2004 which allows a Debtor Company with prospect may continue its business; this principle provided that a bankruptcy does not by law make the company dissolve. Pursuant to Article 104 paragraph (1) of Law No. 37/2004, the business continuity of a bankrupt company depends on the Curator's perspective on the business prospect of the bankrupt debtor in the future. By considering the Article 104 paragraph (1) of Law No. 37/2004 and the Business Continuity Principle, Curator along with the Creditor Committee with the approval from the Supervisory Judge, may propose so that the company that has been declared bankrupt and insolvent may still operate its business.

[125] Buying shares of a company that have gone into insolvency and dissolved is not possible. Meanwhile buying shares on a company that has gone into insolvency but still operates its business is possible, but there are several considerations that the buyer should think of, such as whether the company will be able to continue its business and earn a profit.

Choice of Law

[126] There is no specific regulation concerning choice of law in Indonesia; choice of law is recognized in Indonesia based on doctrines *Lex loci contractus* (law of the place where the contract is made), *Lex loci solutionis* (law of the place where relevant performance occurs), the proper law of the contract and the most characteristic connection. At the same time, the principle source of the law of arbitration in Indonesia is Law No. 30/1999. According to Law No. 30/1999, a dispute is arbitrable only if that dispute is of a commercial nature (i.e., commerce, banking, finance, capital investment, industry and IPR) and concerns rights which, as a matter of law and regulation, fall within the full legal authority of the disputing parties. In addition, arbitration is not permitted for matter which, as a matter of law, may not be settled privately.

[127] Moreover, a written arbitration agreement obviates the rights or the parties to bring dispute in the District Courts, which would otherwise have jurisdiction over civil dispute. The District Courts have no authority to hear disputes where parties are bound by an arbitration agreement and are required to reject and not participate in the resolution of disputes which already have been adjudicated by arbitration, except in limited circumstances as provided in the Law No. 30/1999.

[128] International Arbitration Awards will only be recognized and may be enforced in the jurisdiction of the Republic of Indonesia if they fulfil the following criteria:

(a) the International Arbitration Award is rendered by an arbitrator or arbitration panel in a country which is bound to the Republic of Indonesia by a bilateral or multilateral treaty on the recognition and enforcement of International Arbitration Awards;

(b) the International Arbitration Awards are limited to awards which are included within the scope of commercial law under Indonesian law;
(c) the International Arbitration Awards, which may only be enforced in Indonesia, are limited to those which do not conflict with public order;
(d) an International Arbitration Award may be enforced in Indonesia after obtaining a writ of execution from the Chairman of the Central Jakarta District Court; and
(e) the International Arbitration Awards, which involve the State of the Republic of Indonesia as one of the parties to the dispute, may only be enforced after obtaining an *exequatur* from the Supreme Court of the Republic of Indonesia, which will then delegate it to the Central Jakarta District Court.

[129] According to the principle of freedom of contract, the parties may conclude an agreement based on consent of the parties as long as it satisfies the following conditions: (a) there must be consent of the individuals who are bound thereby; (b) there must be capacity to conclude an agreement; (c) there must be a specific subject; (d) there must be an admissible cause. Therefore, contractual agreement which is subject to the law of a different jurisdiction is recognized as long as fulfil those requirements.

Process

Process: Merger

[130] Law No. 40/2007 devotes a special section to mergers, consolidation, and acquisitions.

[131] Law No. 40/2007 applies to listed (public) PT unless otherwise regulated in prevailing laws and regulations in the capital market sector. Further, provision on responsibilities of directors and/or commissioners resulting from their fault or negligence under this law are without prejudice to the prevailing regulations on criminal law.

[132] One or more companies may merge with another existing company or may consolidate with another company and form a new company. Merger and consolidation results in the dissolution of the merging or consolidating company without prior liquidation process.

[133] The plan for the consolidation or merger must be set out in the plan for consolidation or merger that is jointly composed by the boards of directors of the merging or consolidating companies and the board of directors of the company that will result from the merger or consolidation, and must contain, at least:

(a) the names and legal domicile of each company that will be merged or consolidated;
(b) the reason for the merger of consolidation as given by the board of directors of the respective companies to be consolidated or merged, and the conditions for consolidation or merger;

(c) the method of valuation and conversion of shares of the respective companies that will be merged or consolidated, in exchange for the shares of the company that will result from the merger or consolidation;
(d) the proposed amendments to the articles of association of the company resulting from the merger or consolidation, if any;
(e) the financial statements for the last three accounting years of the companies that will be merged or consolidated;
(f) continuous plan or termination of business activities from a company that will be merged or consolidated;
(g) pro forma balance sheet of the company that will result from the merger or consolidation in accordance with generally accepted accounting principles in Indonesia;
(h) the method of settlement of the status, rights, and obligations of employees of the merging or consolidating company;
(i) the method of settlement of rights and obligations of the merging or consolidating company against any third party;
(j) the method of settlement of the rights of shareholders who disapprove the merger or consolidation;
(k) the names of members of the board of directors and commissioners as well as their salary, remuneration and allowance for the members of the board of directors and commissioners of the company that will result from the merger or consolidation;
(l) the proposed timeframe for the implementation of the merger or consolidation;
(m) a report on the situation, development and result achieved by each company that will be merged or consolidated;
(n) the main business activity of each company that will be merged or consolidated and every change that occurs within the current accounting year; and
(o) details on issues which occurred within the current accounting year which may affect the business of the company that will be merged or consolidated.

[134] The merger or consolidation can be carried out only if the plan for merger or consolidation is approved by the GMS of the respective companies.

Process: Acquisition

[135] The takeover of a company can be carried out by acquisition of shares which have been issued by the company and/or shares that will be issued by the company through the board of directors of the relevant company or directly through the shareholders, with the result that there is a transfer of control of the company.

[136] The takeover of a company can be carried out by a legal entity or an individual. If the takeover is to be carried out by a company, the board of directors must ensure that before implementing the takeover plan, it is carried out based on a GMS which is attended by at least three-quarters of the total shares having valid voting rights and approved by at least three-quarters of the total votes validly cast in the meeting.

[137] If the takeover is carried out through the board of directors, the acquiring party must notify its intention to the board of directors of the company to be acquired. The board of directors of the company to be acquired and the board of directors of the acquiring company, with the approval from each of their respective boards of commissioners, have to compose an acquisition plan which must contain, at least:

(a) the names and legal domicile of the acquiring company and the company to be acquired;
(b) the reason for the acquisition as given by the board of directors of the acquiring company and the company to be acquired;
(c) the financial statements for the last accounting year of the acquiring company and the company to be acquired;
(d) the method of valuation and conversion of shares of the company to be acquired against the shares in exchange, in the event that payment for the acquisition is made in shares;
(e) the amount of shares to be acquired;
(f) preparation of fund;
(g) pro forma consolidated balance sheets of the acquiring company following the acquisition, in accordance with the generally accepted accounting principle in Indonesia;
(h) the method of settlement of the rights of shareholders who disapprove the acquisition;
(i) the method of settlement of status, rights, and obligations of members of the board of directors, commissioners, and employees of the company that will be acquired;
(j) the proposed timeframe for the implementation of acquisition, including the period for authorization of share transfer from the shareholders to the board of directors of the relevant company;
(k) the proposed amendments to the articles of association of the company resulting from the acquisition, if any.

[138] If the acquisition is carried out directly through the shareholders, the above-listed provisions are not required. Direct acquisition through shareholders must take into account relevant provisions under the articles of association of the company to be acquired, in particular regarding the transfer of rights over shares, and other agreements entered between the respective company and any third party.

Matters to Be Taken into Account with Regard to Merger, Consolidation, and Acquisition

[139] In the legal actions of merger, consolidation, and acquisition, a company must take into account:

(a) the interests of the company, minority shareholders, and employees;

(b) the interests of the creditors and other business partners of the company; and
(c) the interests of the public and fair competition in running the business.

[140] Shareholders who disapprove the GMS decision with respect to the merger, consolidation or acquisition have the right to ask the company to purchase their shares at a fair price, provided however that such purchase does not violate the provision on repurchase of shares by a company under Law No. 40/2007 as follows:

(a) a repurchase of shares that have been issued must not cause the net assets of the company to be less than the issued capital plus mandatory reserve capital; and
(b) the total nominal value of the repurchased shares and pledged shares or fiduciary security over shares of the company and/or any other company whose shares are owned directly or indirectly by the company, must not exceed 10% of the total issued shares of the company, unless stipulated otherwise under the capital market regulations.

[141] If the shares to be repurchased exceed the above limitation, the company must ensure that the remaining shares are purchased by a third party. The implementation of the above shareholders rights, however, does not stop the process of merger, consolidation or acquisition.

The Procedures of Merger, Consolidation, and Acquisition

[142] The decision of a GMS with respect to the merger, consolidation or acquisition of a company is valid if taken in accordance with the following:

(a) The directors of the relevant company must publish the summary of the merger, consolidation or acquisition plan in at least one Indonesian daily newspaper having national circulation and must notify its employees in writing no later than thirty days prior to the summons of GMS with respect to such merger, consolidation or acquisition. The announcement must also contain information to the effect that any concerned parties may obtain the merger, consolidation or acquisition plan in the office of the company from the date of the announcement until the date of the GMS.
(b) The creditors may submit objections to the company within fourteen days from the announcement of the merger, consolidation or acquisition plan. If no creditors have submitted an objection to the plan within such period, the creditors are deemed to approve the merger, consolidation or acquisition plan.
(c) Any objection from the creditors that cannot be settled by the board of directors within fourteen days from the announcement on the merger, consolidation or acquisition plan must be submitted to the GMS for settlement. Until

settlement can be achieved, the merger, acquisition or consolidation cannot be implemented.

[143] The obligation to publish the summary of the proposed acquisition in at least one Indonesian daily newspaper having a national circulation and the obligation to notify the employees in writing within thirty days before the summons of GMS also applies in the case of direct acquisition from the shareholders.

Amendments to the Articles of Association or Report with Regard to Merger, Consolidation, or Acquisition

[144] The merger, consolidation or acquisition plan that has obtained the approval of the GMS must be made into a merger, consolidation or acquisition deed, which is made before a notary in Indonesian language.

[145] Copies of the merger deed must be attached to the request for amendment of the articles of association of the company in order to get the approval from and/or to be reported to the MOLHR. The merger deed, whether or not accompanied by an amendment to the articles of association, must be reported to the MOLHR to be recorded in the company registry.

[146] In order to receive authorization from the MOLHR, copies of a consolidation deed must be attached to the request for authorization of the deed of establishment of the company resulting from the consolidation.

[147] Copies of an acquisition deed must be attached to the request for amendment of the articles of association of the company in order to be reported to the MOLHR. If the acquisition is carried out directly from the shareholders, copies of the deed of transfer of shares must be attached to the report to MOLHR on the change of composition of shareholders.

[148] Every amendment of the articles of association of the company resulting from a merger, consolidation or acquisition must also be recorded in the company registry and announced in the supplement to the State Gazette of the Republic of Indonesia.

[149] An acquisition made directly through the shareholders must be stated in a deed of transfer in the form of a notarial deed in the Indonesian language. Further, a copy of the deed of transfer of shares must be attached to the submission of notification to the MOLHR in respect of the change of composition of shareholders following the acquisition.

Dissolution of a Company as a Result of Merger or Consolidation

[150] When there is a merger or consolidation, the company that was consolidated or merged is dissolved provided that:

(a) the assets and liabilities of the company that is merged or that has been consolidated must, by application of law, be transferred to the company resulting from the merger or consolidation; and
(b) the shareholders of the company that was merged or that was consolidated become shareholders of the company resulting from the merger or consolidation.

Announcement of Merger or Consolidation

[151] The board of directors of the company formed as a result of a merger or consolidation must publish the results of the merger or consolidation in one or more daily newspapers not later than thirty days from the date that the consolidation or merger is completed. This applies to the board of directors of the company that has implemented a takeover.

[152] The publication is to inform interested third parties as to what has been done with respect to the merger or consolidation or takeover. This publication is made within thirty days from:

(a) the approval of the MOLHR of alteration of the articles of association in the case of a merger;
(b) the receipt of the report by the MOLHR, either with respect to alteration in the articles of association or when there were no accompanying alterations in the articles of association;
(c) the authorization of the MOLHR of the deed of establishment of the company in the case of a consolidation.

[153] Under the Company Law the merger, consolidation or takeover of a company is further governed by Government Regulation Number 27 of 1998 dated 24 February 1998 on Merger, Consolidation, and Acquisition of PT ('*GR No. 27/1998*').

Separation or Segregation

[154] Law No. 40/2007 stipulates a new provision on separation or segregation that was not provided in the previous law. The corporate action of a separation or segregation may be carried out by the following ways:

(a) Pure segregation, which results in the transfer by law of all the assets and liabilities of the company to two or more companies receiving such transfer, where the company that conducted the segregation will be dissolved by law. In this case, no deed of transfer is required.
(b) Non-pure segregation, commonly known as a 'spin-off', which results in the transfer by law of some part of the assets and liabilities of the company to one or more companies receiving such transfer, where the company that conducted the spin-off will remain in existence.

[155] Further stipulations concerning separation or segregation shall be provided in a government regulation that has not been issued to date.

Government Regulation No. 27 of 1998 Dated 24 February 1998 on Merger, Consolidation, and Acquisition of PT

[156] GR No. 27/1998 applies to the merger, consolidation or acquisition of a company without prejudice to other regulations and legislation relating specifically to the merger, consolidation, and acquisition of a company. In principle, legal actions in the context of acquisition, merger or consolidation of a company, must abide by this regulation, unless there are special provisions such as those relating to banking and the capital market. Pursuant to Law No. 40/2007, implementing regulations of Law No. 1/1995 on PT shall remain valid as long as it is not contrary to, or has not been replaced pursuant to, Law No. 40/2007. Based on such provision, GR No. 27/1998, as the implementing regulations on merger, consolidation, and acquisition of PT will remain valid, provided, however, that certain adjustments with the Law No. 40/2007 will be required, in particular regarding the announcement of the proposed merger, consolidation, or acquisition and notification to the employees of the acquired company, which shall be made thirty days before the summons of the GMS.

[157] The existence of the PT in the business world is very important and strategic for directing development activities in the face of the process of globalization and liberalization of the world economy. It is important, however, that a merger, consolidation or acquisition of a company which may lead to monopoly or to unfair competition, must be avoided from the outset. The Company Law outlines the principles which apply to the merger, consolidation or acquisition of a PT, and more specific conditions and procedures are stipulated by government regulation. The regulation covers issues such as the conditions and procedures applying to a merger, consolidation or acquisition, preparation of a merger, consolidation or acquisition plan, the obligation to announce, notification of employees, lodging of objections to the plan and the right to apply for the cancellation of the proposed merger, consolidation or acquisition.

[158] Merger and consolidation must be carried out without a liquidation process beforehand. The government regulation confirms that a merger or consolidation process performed without prior liquidation will have the following legal result:

(a) the shareholders of the merging company or the consolidating company become the shareholders of the company 'receiving' the merger or the company formed by the consolidation;
(b) the assets and liabilities of the merging or consolidating company are, by operation of law, transferred to the company receiving the merger or the company resulting from the consolidation.

Conditions for Merger, Consolidation, or Acquisition of PT under Government Regulation No. 27/1998 jo. Law No. 40/2007

[159] The merger, consolidation, and acquisition can only be carried out by taking into consideration:

(a) the company's interests, minority shareholders, and employees concerned;
(b) public interests and sound competition in the running of business.

[160] In the Article 126 paragraph (1) of Law No. 40/2007, besides merger, consolidation, and acquisition, demerger is also added. In addition, it must as well consider about creditors and other business partners of the company.

[161] A merger, consolidation or acquisition does not reduce the minority shareholders' rights to sell their shares at a proper price. A shareholder who does not agree with the resolution of the GMS on the merger, consolidation or acquisition can reserve his or her right to demand that the shares he or she owns be sold at an appropriate price in accordance with the provisions in Article 55 of Law No. 1/1995 which has been replaced by Article 62 paragraph (1) of Law No. 40/2007. The use of this right does not stop the process of implementation of the merger, consolidation or acquisition.

[162] The merger, consolidation or acquisition must also take the creditors' interests into account. In this case creditors are the creditors of the company to merge or to consolidate or to acquire and to be acquired.

[163] The merger, consolidation or acquisition can only be carried out with the approval from the GMS by virtue of a resolution of the GMS, attended by the shareholders representing at least three-quarters of the total number of shares with voting rights and approved by at least three-quarters of the total votes. For a public PT, the requirements for attendance and decision-making are determined in accordance with the regulations and legislation applicable to the capital markets.

Procedures for Mergers, Consolidations, or Acquisitions under Government Regulation No. 27/1998 jo. Law No. 40/2007

Merger

[164] The boards of directors of the company to merge and of the company to receive the merger must each prepare a proposal for the planned merger.

[165] The proposals must receive approval from the boards of directors and at least contain:

(a) the name and domicile of the company to merge;
(b) the reasons for, and explanation of the board of directors of the company to merge, and the conditions of the merger;
(c) the procedures for conversion of the shares of each company into the shares of the company resulting from the merger;
(d) the draft amendments to the articles of association of the company resulting from the merger;
(e) the balance sheets, profit and loss statements for the last three fiscal years of all the companies to merge; and
(f) items deemed to be known by each shareholder of each company, *inter alia*:
  (i) a pro forma balance sheet of the company resulting from the merger in accordance with accountancy standards, an estimation of profit and loss, the prospects for the company after the merger based on evaluations made by independent experts;
  (ii) proposals for the position of employees of the company to merge;
  (iii) proposals for dealing with the company's rights and obligations to third parties;
  (iv) proposals for dealing with the rights of shareholders who do not agree with the merger of the company;
  (v) the organization, salaries and other allowances for the board of directors and the board of commissioners of the company resulting from the merger;
  (vi) an estimation of the time for implementation of the merger;
  (vii) a report on the situation and operations of the company and the results achieved;
  (viii) the main activities of the company and amendments during the current fiscal year;
  (ix) the specification of problems arising during the current fiscal year;
  (x) the names of members of the board of directors and the board of commissioners; and
  (xi) the salaries and other allowances for the members of the board of directors and the board of commissioners.

Whereas under Law No. 40/2007, the proposal is regulated as stated in point [133] above.

[166] If the company to merge is bound to one group or multiple groups, the proposed merger plan must contain a consolidated balance sheet and pro forma balance sheet for the company resulting from the merger. The proposal will constitute data for preparing the draft of the merger plan jointly formulated by the boards of directors of the company to merge. The draft must at least contain the items stipulated in the proposed plan for the merger as stated in *Article 123 paragraph (2) of Law No. 40/2007*.

[167] The draft merger plan must also contain confirmation from the company to receive the merger of the acceptance of the transfer of all the rights and obligations of the company to merge. The summary of the merger plan must be published by the board of directors in two daily papers and be notified in writing to the employees of the company which is to merge at least fourteen days before the summons to a GMS. Whereas, Article 127 paragraph (2) of Law No. 40/2007 simplified the requirements that the summary of the merger plan must be published by the board of directors in *one newspaper* and be notified in writing to the employees of the company which is to merge *at least thirty days* before the summons to a GMS.

[168] Approval for the merger plan, together with the draft of the merger deed, must be obtained from the GMS of each company. The approved draft of the merger plan deed must be in the Indonesian language and executed in the presence of a notary.

[169] If the merger of the company is carried out without an amendment of the articles of association, the merger will come into force as from the date of approval by the MOLHR for amendment of the articles of association. If the merger of the company is carried out together with an amendment of the articles of association which does not require approval from the MOLHR, then the merger will come into force as from the date of registration of the merger deed and the amendment deed of the articles of association in the company registry. If the merger of the company is carried out without an amendment deed of the articles of association, then the merger will come into force as from the date of signing of the merger deed. Whereas under Law No. 40/2007, if the merger of the company is carried out with an amendment of the articles of association that need Minister's approval, the merger will come into force as from the date of approval by the MOLHR for amendment of the articles of association or a later date determined in the Minister's approval which is the date after the date of Minister's approval. If the merger of the company is carried out together with an amendment of the articles of association which does not require approval from the MOLHR, then the merger will come into force as from the date of notification of the amendment of the articles of association is received by the MOLHR, or a later date determined in the deed of merger which is a date that had been agreed by parties and is the date after the date of acceptance of amendment of articles of association's notification by Minister. If the merger of the company is carried out without an amendment deed of the articles of association, then the merger will come into force as from the date of recording of merger in Company Registry by MOLHR.

[170] If the merger of the company is carried out through an amendment of the articles of association, the board of directors of the company to receive the merger must submit an application for amendment to the articles of association to the MOLHR. After receiving approval from the MOLHR, the board must then register it in the company registry and publish notification of it in the supplement to the Indonesian state gazette. If the merger of the company is carried out together with an amendment of the articles of association, the board of directors of the company to receive the merger have to report the merger deed of the company and the amendment deed of the articles of association to the MOLHR. The board must also register the company in the company registry and publish notification of the merger in the supplement to the Indonesian state gazette. Whereas under Law No. 40/2007, if the merger of the company is carried out through an amendment of the articles of association *that requires Minister's approval*, the board of directors of the company to receive the merger must submit an application for approval of amendment to the articles of association to the MOLHR. If the merger of the company is carried out together with an amendment of the articles of association *which does not require approval from the MOLHR*, the board of directors of the company to receive the merger has to report the merger deed of the company and the amendment deed of the articles of association to the MOLHR.

[171] The application for approval of the MOLHR as outlined above must be submitted in writing to the MOLHR by attaching the deed of amendment of the articles of association and the merger deed. The approval is given at the latest sixty days after receipt of the application. If the application is refused, the refusal is notified to the applicant in writing, stating the reasons therefore, within a period of sixty days. Whereas under Law No. 40/2007 provides procedures for the electronic:

(1) submission of applications for and the granting of ratification of legal entity status;
(2) submission of applications for and the granting of approval for the amendment of articles of association;
(3) delivery of notifications and receipt of notifications of amendments to articles of association and/or notification of and receipt of notification of other changes to data by legal entity administration system information technology services besides manual systems still being possible in certain circumstances.

Furthermore, Law No. 40/2007 and the implementing regulation is silent regarding when the applications for and the granting of approval for the amendment of articles of association and notifications and receipt of notifications of amendments to articles of association and/or notification of and receipt of notification of other changes to data is given by MOLHR. In practice the MOLHR give the approval approximately two to three days after receipt of the application is considered complete.

[172] The application for approval of amendment of the articles of association or the submission of the report on the merger deed of the company and amendment deed of the articles of association must be carried out no later than fourteen days after the resolution of the GMS. If the merger of the company is carried out through an amendment of the articles of association, then the company to merge is dissolved as from the date of the approval for amendment to the articles of association by the MOLHR. If the merger of the company is carried out together with an amendment of the articles of association, then the company to merge is merged as from the date of the registration of the merger deed and the amendment deed of the articles of association in the company registry. Whereas under Law No. 40/2007, the application for approval of amendment of the articles of association or the submission of the report on the merger deed of the company and amendment deed of the articles of association must be carried out no later than thirty days as of the date of notary deed containing amendment of articles of association. If the merger of the company is carried out through an amendment of the articles of association which requires approval from Minister, then the company to merge is dissolved as from the date of the approval for amendment to the articles of association by the MOLHR or a later date determined in the Minister's approval. If the merger of the company is carried out together with an amendment of the articles of association which does not require approval from Minister, then the company to merge is merged as from the date notification of the amendment of the articles of association is received by the Minister, or a later date determined in the deed of merger.

[173] If the merger of the company is carried out without the amendment of the articles of association, then the company to merge is merged as from the date of the execution of the merger deed. Whereas under Law No. 40/2007, if the merger of the company is carried out without the amendment of the articles of association, the copy of deed of merger shall be submitted to the MOLHR to be registered in the company registry, then the company to merge is merged as from the date of receipt of notification of the amendments of the company's data which do not constitute amendments of the articles of association.

[174] As from the date of the signing of the merger deed the board of directors of the company to merge must not take any legal action unless deemed necessary in the context of the implementation of the merger. Any breach of this obligation is the responsibility of the board of directors of the company concerned.

Consolidation

[175] The above provisions related to mergers are similarly valid for consolidations. The founders of the company resulting from consolidation will be the companies wishing to consolidate. The shareholders of the company to be founded will be the shareholders of the company wishing to consolidate. The assets of the company to be founded will be the entire assets of the company wishing to consolidate. In this case, 'the assets' refers to the total assets of the company contained in the assets column of the latest balance sheet approved by the GMS.

[176] The consolidation deed will become the basis for formulating the deed of establishment of the consolidated company. The board of directors of the consolidating company has to submit an application for legalization of the deed of establishment of the consolidated company to the MOLHR, no later than fourteen days after the date of resolution of the GMS. After receiving approval from the

MOLHR, the board must register the company in the company registry and publish notification of the registration in the supplement to the state gazette. The application for legalization of the deed of establishment must be submitted in writing to the MOLHR by attaching the consolidation deed. The MOLHR must then legalize the application no later than sixty days after receiving the application. If the application is refused, the refusal will be notified to the applicant in writing, stating the reasons for such refusal. Whereas under Law No. 40/2007 the obligation to register the company in the company registry is already included on the same date as the date of:

(a) the Ministerial Decree regarding the ratification of the company's legal entity status, the approval for the amendment of the articles of association for which approval is necessary;
(b) receipt of notification of the amendments to the articles of association for which approval is not necessary; or
(c) receipt of notification of the amendments of the company's data which do not constitute amendments of the articles of association.

[177] The consolidating company will be dissolved as from the date of legalization of the deed of establishment of the consolidated company by the MOLHR. As from the date of the signing of the consolidation deed, the board of directors of the merging companies must not take any legal action unless deemed necessary in the context of the implementation of the consolidation. Any breach of this obligation is the liability of the board of directors of the company concerned.

Acquisition

[178] *In the event that the acquisition is performed through the board of directors*, the party wishing to acquire must notify its intent to the board of directors of the company to be acquired. The board of directors of the company to be acquired and the party wishing to acquire shall then respectively prepare a proposal for the plan of acquisition.

[179] The proposals must receive approval from the boards of directors of both companies, and must at least contain:

(a) the name and domicile of the company and other legal body, or identity of the individual to acquire;
(b) the reasons for and explanations of each of the board of directors of the acquiring company or the management of the acquiring legal entity or the acquiring individual;
(c) an annual report, especially the annual calculation of the latest fiscal year of the company and the other legal body to carry out the acquisition;
(d) the acquisition procedures for conversion of the shares of each of the companies, if payment for the acquisition is to be made using shares;
(e) a draft amendment of the articles of association of the company resulting from the acquisition;

(f) the total shares to be acquired;
(g) the availability of funds;
(h) a pro forma joint balance sheet of the company resulting from the acquisition, prepared in accordance with financial accounting standards, an estimation of profit and loss, and the prospects of the company based on evaluations made by independent experts;
(i) proposals for dealing with the rights of shareholders who do not agree with the acquisition of the company;
(j) proposals for dealing with the employees of the company to be acquired;
(k) an estimation of the time for implementation of the acquisition.

Whereas under Law No. 40/2007, the proposal is regulated as stated in point [137] above.

[180] As far as procedure is concerned, an acquisition is carried out by the boards of directors of the company to be acquired and that of the acquiring party.

[181] The proposal will constitute data for the preparation of the acquisition deed to be jointly formulated by the boards of directors of both companies. The draft must contain at least the items stipulated in the proposed plan for the acquisition as set out above. The summary of the draft proposal for acquisition must be published by the boards of directors in two daily papers, and the employees of the company wishing to acquire must be notified in writing, at least fourteen days before the summons for a GMS of each company. The draft amendment to the articles of association of the company, in this case, shall be attached only if the proposal for the acquisition requires an amendment to the articles of association. The acquisition draft must receive approval from the GMS of the company to be acquired and the acquiring company or a similar body of the acquiring party. Whereas under Law No. 40/2007 the summary of the draft proposal for acquisition must be published by the boards of directors in *at least one* daily newspaper, and the employees of the company wishing to acquire must be notified in writing, at least *thirty* days before the summons for a GMS of each company.

[182] The approved draft of acquisition must be incorporated into the acquisition deed. The acquisition deed must be made in the presence of a notary and in the Indonesian language.

[183] If the acquisition of the company is carried out through an amendment of the articles of association, the acquisition will come into force as from the date of approval of the amendment to the articles of association by the MOLHR. If the acquisition of the company is carried out together with an amendment of the articles of association which does not require approval from the MOLHR, then the acquisition will come into force as from the date of registration of the acquisition deed in the companies register. If the acquisition of the company is carried out without causing amendment to the articles of association, then the acquisition will come into force as from the date of signing of the acquisition deed. Whereas under Law No. 40/2007 if the acquisition of the company is carried out through an amendment of the articles of association, the acquisition will come into force as from the date of approval of the amendment to the articles of association by the

MOLHR. If the acquisition of the company is carried out together with an amendment of the articles of association which does not require approval from the MOLHR, then the acquisition will come into force as from the date of notification of the amendment of the articles of association is received by MOLHR, or later date determined in the deed of acquisition which is a date that had been agreed by parties and is the date of acceptance of amendment of articles of association's notification by MOLHR. If the acquisition of the company is carried out without causing amendment to the articles of association, the copy of deed of acquisition shall be submitted to the MOLHR to be registered in the company registry, then the acquisition will come into force as from the date of receipt of notification of the amendments of the company's data which do not constitute amendments of the articles of association.

Objection to Merger, Consolidation, or Acquisition of Companies

[184] The boards of directors of the respective companies must publish the summary of merger, consolidation or acquisition plan in at least one Indonesian daily newspaper having national circulation and notify its employees in writing within thirty days prior to the summons of GMS with respect to such merger, consolidation or acquisition. The announcement must also contain information that any concerned parties may obtain the merger, consolidation or acquisition plan in the office of the company from the date of announcement until the date of the GMS.

[185] The creditors may submit objections to the company within fourteen days from the announcement of the merger, consolidation or acquisition plan. If no creditors have submitted any objection to the plan within such period, the creditors are deemed to approve the merger, consolidation or acquisition plan. Any objection from the creditors that cannot be settled by the board of directors within fourteen days as of the announcement on the merger, consolidation or acquisition plan must be submitted to the GMS for settlement. The merger, acquisition or consolidation cannot be implemented prior to such settlement.

Other Provisions

[186] The board of directors of the company resulting from the merger or consolidation must announce the results of the merger or consolidation in two daily papers no later than thirty days after the date the merger or consolidation takes effect. This provision also applies to the board of directors of a company having assets in the acquiring company. Announcement in this case is made by the acquiring party. The value of the company's assets is stipulated by a Ministerial Decree. Whereas under Law No. 40/2007 the board of directors of the company resulting from the merger or consolidation must announce the results of the merger, acquisition or consolidation in one daily newspaper or mores no later than thirty days after the date the merger or consolidation takes effect.

[187] In performing its duties, in the context of merger, consolidation or acquisition, the board of directors of the company must act exclusively in the interests of the company. If there is a conflict of interests between the company and the board of directors, the board must reveal this in a proposal for the plan or draft of the merger, consolidation or acquisition. This also applies to the board of commissioners.

Mergers and Acquisitions under Law No. 8/1995 on the Capital Market

[188] Public takeovers are regulated under OJK Regulation No. 9/POJK.04/2018 on Takeover of Public Companies. Mergers are regulated under OJK Regulation No. 74/POJK.04/2016 on Mergers or Consolidations of Public Company *jo.* OJK Regulation No. 58/POJK.04/2017 on the Electronic Submission of Registration Statements and Applications for Corporate Actions. Since 2013, the competent authority that is able to regulate the public takeovers on Capital Market is OJK.

[189] The aforementioned rules are applicable to all public companies that are also listed on the IDX.

[190] The most common method for acquiring a public company in Indonesia is by way of a direct acquisition in which the existing shares are directly acquired from the shareholders.

[191] Beside the common method of acquisition as mentioned above, there is the indirect acquisition in which the board of directors is involved, and investors can acquire a shareholding, such as:

(a) debt-to-equity swap;
(b) private placement; or
(c) rights issue.

Debt-to-Equity Swap

[192] By performing debt-to-equity swap, it will benefit the target company through the boost to cash flow that resulted from the reduction or elimination of financing ongoing principal repayments and interest costs. However, it may become a disadvantage for the existing shareholders of the target company, considering that the equity that used in debt-to-equity swap is originated from the portfolio capital of the target company. Therefore, the shares of the existing shareholders will be diluted (the shares value decline).

Private Placement

[193] The advantages of the private placement are:

(i) The procedure is faster and cost-effective. It is because the target company may offer the shares without registration to the OJK.

(ii) Choice of investors. Since the private placement is only offered on limited numbers of investors, therefore the target company may choose the investors.

[194] The disadvantage of the private placement is the limited investors or the difficulty to find the investor. It is because the offer is not performed through the registration to the OJK. Therefore, there is no announcement on the offering. This can lead to the target company facing difficulty in finding the investor.

Rights Issue

[195] The advantage of the right issue is the shares that are sold in right issue usually has cheaper price than the existing shares. However, it may be a disadvantage for the shareholder that did not buy the shares (using the pre-emptive right), because the shares of them may become diluted.

[196] The director of the target company's responsibilities on receiving a takeover offer are:

(a) In doing such action, the directors shall comply with the interest, objective and the purpose of the target company (Fiduciary Duty/Article 92 paragraph (1) of Law No. 40/2007).
(b) The directors shall inform the offer to the shareholders of the target company.

[197] In terms of the acquisition is performed through the directors, the directors may decline the acquisition offer from the directors of the acquiring company. However, in terms of the acquisition is performed through the shareholders, the directors do not have any action to resist the change of control.

[198] In relation to the partial offer there is a possibility for a buyer to make a partial offer. As mentioned before on the takeover structure, the acquiring company may offer the acquired company to buy their share in amount of partial (not full). As long as, it is still considered as majority shares (controlling) of the acquired company, the transaction will be considered as an acquisition. This partial offer may be performed through the 'voluntary' bid in the Stock Exchange by the company (OJK Regulation No. 54/POJK.04/2015). This method may help the company to make partial offer on shares of the targeted company in the Stock Exchange, in case, the company cannot approach the targeted company outside from the Stock Exchange.

[199] Mandatory Tender Offer ('*MTO*') is regulated under the OJK Regulation No. 9/POJK.04/2018. Considering the acquisition is performed by the public listed company, therefore after establishing the deed of acquisition, the new controlling company shall hold a tender offer for the remaining shares of the acquired company. The MTO is triggered, when the new controlling company acquires 80% of the subscribed shares of the acquired company, therefore the controlling company is required to hold the MTO in order to transfer at least 20% of shares of the acquired company to be owned by the public. In addition, the MTO gives rights to the shareholders of the acquired company to sell their shares to the public through the bid.

[200] The applicable regulations on the purchase of shares in advance or during a bid are:

(a) OJK Regulation No. 32/POJK.04/2015 on Capital Increasement of Public Company by Giving the Right Issues or Pre-emptive Rights (*Hak Memesan Efek Terlebih Dahulu*). This regulation regulates the pre-emptive right in terms of the rights issue that is given to the existing shareholders with a certain ratio of their share ownership percentage with regards to the capital increasement in the public company. The pre-emptive right is given to the existing shareholders in order to buy the shares in advance of the rights issue. It is intended to prevent the shares of the existing shareholders to be deluded.

(b) OJK Regulation No. 54/POJK.04/2015 on the Voluntary Tender Offer. This regulation regulates the voluntary tender offer in order to perform the takeover on the target company. It is performed by the acquiring company, if he does not find the target company in order to perform the takeover. Therefore, the acquiring company will perform the offering/bid in the stock exchange in order to find the shareholders of the target company's share.

(c) OJK Regulation No. 9/POJK.04/2018 on the Takeover of Public Company. This regulation regulated the procedure to perform the takeover of the public company in the capital market. There are several conducts that should be perform by the acquiring company, one of it is the mandatory bid that intended to keep the 20% of the shares of the target company is owned by the public.

(d) OJK Regulation No. 11/POJK.04/2017 on Reporting of Substantial Shareholdings in Public Company. This regulation obliges the director or the commissioner of the listed company/public company to report the ownership of the shares to OJK, if there is transaction on the shares.

(e) BAPEPAM Regulation No. IX.E.1: Annex of the Decision of the Head of BAPEPAM No. KEP-412/BL/2009 on the Affiliated Transaction and Conflict of Interest Transaction. This regulation is intended to give legal certainty and protection for the shareholders, especially the independent shareholders related with the transaction that is performed by the listed company or public company with his affiliated or conflict of interest transaction by performing the public announcement of the affiliated transaction.

(f) BAPEPAM Regulation No. IX.E.2: Annex of the Decision of the Head of BAPEPAM No. KEP-614/BL/2011 on the Material Transaction and Amendment of Main Business Activity. This regulation regulates the material transaction that in amount of 20% to 50% of the equity of the company. Since the acquisition shall be performed on the majority shares (in terms through the voluntary bid), therefore, it will be considered as the material transaction. Then, the acquiring company shall perform several conducts that obliged under this regulation before performing the transaction.

[201] According to OJK Regulation No. 11/POJK.04/2017, the director or commissioner of the issuer or public company shall report to the OJK on the ownership and every change of his ownership of the share of the company, at least ten days after the execution of the transaction. This obligation prevails on every party that owned 5% or more of the subscribed capital. A copy of the required report shall be provided by the OJK for public disclosure.

[202] An exclusivity or a break fee is subject to the agreement between the parties, and it is not regulated under the prevailing laws and regulations. In the context of the acquisition, the exclusivity may be given by the target company to the buyer before drafting the Shares Purchase Agreement (PJBS/*Perjanjian Jual Beli Saham*). The commitment of the target company may be obtained by stating the exclusivity in the MoU that agreed by both of the parties.

[203] The constraints on a normal due diligence among others are the documents are incomplete, the permits may be already expired, and the targeted company may undisclose several required documents.

[204] Basically, the due diligence is feasible in the context of a public takeover, both the legal due diligence, operational due diligence and the financial due diligence.

[205] According to OJK Regulation No. 9/POJK.04/2018, permits the acquirer to publicly disclose information on the ongoing negotiations with the selling shareholders related to a takeover, or to keep the information confidential.

[206] The following are the minimum components that must be included in the disclosure obligation:

- Estimates of the amount of shares that will be acquired.
- The identity of the acquirer (name, address, phone number, types of business activity and the purpose of the takeover).
- The amount of securities which have been owned by the acquirer (if any).
- Plan or decision to co-operate between the parties in an organized group for the purpose of the takeover (if any).
- Method and process of the negotiation.
- Content of the negotiation.

Information that must be disclosed following the completion of the takeover includes:

- The amount of shares acquired and the total ownership of shares.
- Identity of the parties (name, address, phone number, types of business activity and the purpose of the takeover).
- Statement that the acquirer is an organized group if that is the case.

[207] In addition, according to OJK Regulation No. 11/POJK.04/2017 on Reporting of Substantial Shareholdings in Public Company. A person who acquires an interest of 5% more of a public listed company (i.e., ultimate beneficial owner) either directly or indirectly is obliged to disclose this interest to the OJK. The publicly-available information to a buyer is in the form of a report that consist of (i) name, domicile, and nationality; (ii) name of the public company; (iii) the amount of shares and the ownership percentage before and after the transactions; (iv) the amount of shares that purchased or sale; (v) the purchase and sale price of each of the shares; (vi) date of transaction; (vii) object of transaction; (viii) the ownership status (direct or indirect); (ix) the identity of the ultimate beneficial owner and the direct shareholder that is registered in the public companies shareholders register on behalf of the ultimate beneficial owner.

[208] If there are undisclosed liabilities in the targeted company, the buyer may protect himself with the confidential agreement that executed before the commencement of the due diligence that stated on the obligation of both parties to disclose every required document. If the confidential agreement is violated, therefore, the buyer may sue the public company through the court.

[209] There is rule applied for any announcements that leaks out in advance regarding the bid, it is considers as insider trading crime in capital market. According to the Article 95 of Law No. 8/1995 on the Capital Market, the insider of the issuer or the public company that has the information shall not perform any purchase or sale on the securities of the concerned issuer or public company or other company that perform transaction with the issuer or public company.

[210] The following individuals will be considered as insiders with respect to insider trading:

- Commissioners, directors or employees of a public company.
- The principal shareholder(s) of a public company.
- Individuals who, due to their position, profession or business relationship with a listed or public company, are able to obtain inside information.
- Parties who, within the last six months of the relevant date, fell into one of the above categories.

[211] In Indonesia, there is no minimum price obligation imposed on a buyer, if the purchase of shares has taken place in advance. Therefore, the seller may determine the minimum price of the shares based on the nominal of the shares or market price.

[212] The securities may be offered as consideration for public takeovers. Instead of using the money, there are several securities that may be offered to the seller in order to buy the shares, which are:

(a) Shares, which are:
  (i) Shares contribution (*Inbreng Saham*)
  This method is performed by transferring the shares of the subsidiary company of the acquiring company as the payment. After the performance of the shares contribution, therefore the target company has become the shareholders on the subsidiary company of the acquiring company.
  (ii) Share swap
  This method is shares exchange between one company and other company. In this method, the exchanged shares are originated from the portfolio of the company that specifically issued for the share swap.

After the share swap transaction, each of the companies has the shares of the other company.

(iii) Shareholders shares Exchange
This method is the exchange on the shares that has been paid up and subscribed by the shareholders.

(b) Bonds
Payments by bonds may be performed in the Combination Based Acquisition, where the payment is performed by the combination of shares, bonds, and assets.

[213] Public takeovers do not have to be offered the same terms to all shareholders. It is because based on the preference of the shareholder. Therefore, in order to pay the acquired company, the acquiring company may have combination of payment method, and it is considered as combination acquisition.

[214] In Indonesia, there is no obligation for the acquiring company to acquire the other classes of security in the target company. However, there are several options or convertible securities that may be offered by the target company to be acquire by the acquiring company, which are:

(a) Assets
The acquiring company may perform the assets acquisition on the target company. This asset may cover the bonds that considered as debt securities.

(b) Convertible bonds
This is a form of securities considered in the gradual acquisition, where the target company may offer the convertible bonds (bonds that may be converted into shares) and the acquiring company may purchase it. In this matter, in the first phase, the acquiring company may give the fund to the target company in order to buy the convertible bonds. Then, on the second phase, the concerned bonds may be converted into the shares of the target company, if the performance of the target company is getting better.

[215] Basically, in the acquisition process, there is no condition from OJK on the financial ability of the acquiring company to acquire the target company. However, in the process of MTO (in terms of the acquiring company will buy the remaining shares), the acquiring company has the obligation to give the proof stating that the new controllers have sufficient funds and offer a full disclosure on the sources of funding. Also, OJK does not have any conditions on the amount of the required finances.

[216] In relation to the timetable, there is a control issue that can affect the time table of public takeover. Wherein companies must submit a notification to the Indonesian Business Competition Supervisory Commission (KPPU) of any takeover which could result in a monopoly or unfair business competition (as determined under the thresholds set out in Government Regulation Number 57 of 2010 on Mergers or Consolidations of Business Entities and Acquisitions of Companies' Shares Which May Result in Monopolistic Practices or Unfair Business Competition ('*GR No. 57/2010*') (*See* below for further information).

[217] In terms of acquisition, the documents that should be reviewed by the regulators are:

(a) Submission of announcement and copy of the acquisition deed (attached on the submission of the announcement) to the Minister of Law and Human Rights.
(b) After the control of the acquired company is success to be taken, therefore the new controlling company shall announce the acquisition to the public and the OJK, at least one working day after the acquisition. By submitting the documents on the information consist of:
  (i) The amount of the acquired shares and total of the ownership of the shares.
  (ii) The personal identity of the acquiring and acquired company.
  (iii) The purpose of controlling.
  (iv) Statement that the new controlling company is an organized group.
  (v) The beneficiary of the Party that carries out the Takeover, if the Party is not a beneficiary.
  (vi) The nature of affiliation with a public company, if there is an affiliate relationship.
  (vii) A description of the approval of the authorized party, if approval is necessary from the authorized party.
(c) In order to perform the MTO, the controlling company shall:
  (i) Submit the announcement text of the transparency information and the support documents to the OJK. The announcement consists of:
    - The background of the acquisition.
    - Information on the shares.
    - Information on the new controller.
    - Information on the acquired company.
    - Contract or activities which have material impact.
    - Terms and conditions of the MTO.
    - The list of names and addresses of the Capital Market Support institution and/or profession that involved in the MTO.
    - Other important information.
  (ii) After the MTO is performed, the controlling company shall submit the report on the result of the MTO to the OJK.

In terms of merger, the relevant requirements are:

(a) Names, domiciles, line of businesses, capital structures and shareholders of any merging or consolidating companies, as well as the details regarding their management and supervisory structures.
(b) Name, domicile, the BOD and BOC composition of the surviving company (for mergers) or of the new company (for consolidations).
(c) Reasons and schedule for the intended merger or consolidation.
(d) Procedures for the conversion of the merging/consolidating companies' shares against the surviving/new company's shares.

(e) Draft amendment of the surviving company's articles of association (if any) or draft of the new company's deed of establishment.
(f) Summary of essential financial data derived from the merging/consolidating companies' audited financial statements for: (a) the last two years (if the companies are public companies); or (b) three years (for private companies which are also participating in the merger/consolidation).
(g) Comparison of financial data from the current interim period with data from the last accounting year's interim period (if any).
(h) Surviving/new company's pro-forma financial information, which has first been reviewed by public accountants.
(i) Summary of an assessor's report pertaining to: (a) the share value of each of the merging/consolidating companies; and (b) the fairness of the merger or consolidation.
(j) Results of an expert assessment of certain aspects of the merger/consolidation (if deemed necessary).
(k) Legal opinion regarding the merger/consolidation.
(l) Procedures to be followed by the merging or consolidating companies when settling any of the following matters:
   (i) Status of their employees;
   (ii) Rights and obligations of any third parties; and
   (iii) Rights of shareholders that may conflict with the merger or consolidation.
(m) Description of the various benefits and risks which may result from the merger or consolidation, along with a mitigation plan and future business plans.

[218] Under OJK Regulation No. 9/POJK.04/2018, there are several required publications related with a MTO, which are:

(a) Acquiring company shall submit the cover letter, announcement on the transparency of information in context of MTO and the supporting documents to the OJK and the targeted company, at least two working days after the announcement of acquisition.
(b) Submit the amendment and/or additional information on the announcement text in context of the MTO and the supporting documents at least five days after receiving the request from the OJK, if the OJK requires the new controlling company to make amendment and/or additional information.
(c) Announce the transparency of information in context of MTO in one daily newspaper that nationally circulated or Stock Exchange's website at least two working days after receiving the letter from the OJK that stated the new controlling company may announce the transparency of information in context of MTO.
(d) Then, after performing the MTO, the acquiring company may submit the report on the result of the MTO to the OJK at least five days after the end of the transaction settlement.

[219] The report on the result of the MTO to OJK must contain at least information about:

(a) the number of shares that must be purchased in the MTO;
(b) MTO implementation period;
(c) the date of completion of the MTO transaction;
(d) list of shareholders who sell their shares;
(e) the number of shares purchased in the implementation of the MTO;
(f) composition of share ownership of the new Controller before and after the MTO.

[220] For the MTO, there is no regulation on the withdrawal. However, if the MTO is withdrawn, the company may be imposed with sanction from the OJK. In other hand, for the 'voluntary' bid, there is the regulation on the withdrawal under the OJK Regulation No. 54/POJK.04/2015, which are:

(a) The 'voluntary' bid may not be withdrawn, if the announcement process has performed, however it may be waived, if the OJK gives the approval.
(b) In terms of the 'voluntary' bid is withdrawn, therefore the offered securities shall be returned at least in twelve days after the withdrawal.

[221] The control on the acquired company will be passed to the buyer, when the deed of the acquisition that made before the notary in Indonesia language, is already informed to the MOLHR.

[222] Before proceeding to the relevant levels of control, the control itself may be defined under the Article 1 point d of Law No. 8/1995, as the ability to determine, booth directly or indirectly, by any methods on the management and/or the policy of the company. Then, exclusively for the public company, under the Article 1 point (4) of the OJK Regulation No. 9/POJK.04/2018, the controller of the public company is:

(a) The party that owned shares more than 50% from the full subscribed capital (*de jure* control).
(b) The party that had the ability to determine the management and/or the policy of the public company, both directly or indirectly (de facto control).

[223] Based on the doctrines, there are several levels of control, which are:

(a) *GMS and Articles of Association:* In the GMS, the party may determine the strategic positions on the management, and also has the ability to amend the articles of association.
(b) *Shares with Special Rights:* The party owns the minority shares in the company. However, he/she has special rights that attached with his shares such as, preferential shares.
(c) *Financial Statements:* If the party consolidate the financial statements of the subsidiary company with the parent company (the controller) in order to

supervise the financial flow from the parent company to the subsidiary company. It is clear that the party is the controller. Because, according to the basic principles of accountancy, if the company has 50% of shares in other company, therefore, the financial statements will be automatically consolidated with the financial statements of the parent company.

[224] There are two ways for squeezing out recalcitrant or dissenting minority shareholders, which are:

(a) Freeze out
Freeze out is the method of the majority shareholders to force the minority shareholder out from the company, by eliminating their status as the minority shareholders. The freeze out may be performed after the acquiring company has controlled the majority shares of the target company. In other countries, the freeze out may be legally performed by particular procedures, such as reverse shares fraction by increasing the nominal value of the shares through the amendment of the articles of association, therefore a large number of shares is exchanged with one shares. As the consequence of this amendment, the minority shareholder hold the fraction of shares, therefore they will be forced to sell their shares.

(b) Squeeze out
The squeeze out is similar with the freeze out and similarly has the element of coercion in order to take out the minority shareholder from the target company. However, in the freeze out, the coercion is directly performed and in the squeeze out, the coercion is indirectly performed. For example, after the acquiring company controls the majority shares, they may manipulate the management of the target company in order to create an unpleasant condition for the minority shareholders, therefore the minority shareholders may choose to sell their shares. Then, the shareholders have a right to be bought out, in terms of their disagreement with the decision of the GMS for acquisition. The right may allow the shareholder to request the company to buy their shares with a reasonable price, with condition, if the acquisition is causing loss to the shareholders. (Article 62 of Law No. 40/2007).

[225] Under the OJK Regulation No. 9/POJK.04/2018, the sanctions on the violation on the rules of the public takeovers under this regulation is an administration sanction issued by OJK, including:

(a) Written warning.
(b) Fines namely the obligation to pay a certain amount of money.
(c) Limitation of business activities.
(d) Suspension of business activities.
(e) Revocation of business license.
(f) Cancellation of approval; and/or
(g) Cancellation of Registration.

[226] Concerning the compliance with the takeover rules, it cannot be enforced through the courts. Therefore, the aforementioned sanctions are the only resort to forcing the company to comply with the takeovers rules.

Process

[227] Mergers and acquisitions involving public companies will, in principle, be subject to the general provisions applicable to PT. This includes specific provisions on mergers and acquisitions as set out in the respective articles of association of the companies involved.

[228] The Capital Market Law contains the following general provisions relating to consolidation, merger, and acquisition:

(1) The OJK (previously Capital Market Supervisory Agency and Financial Institution BAPEPAM & LK) can obligate issuers or public companies to grant a pre-emptive right to every shareholder proportionally if the issuers or public company issued shares or stocks that can be exchanged with the shares of the issuers or public companies.
(2) OJK can obligate issuers or public companies to obtain the majority approval of independent shareholders if the issuers or public companies conduct a 'Conflict of Interest Transaction', which is a transaction in which the economic interest of the issuers or public companies conflict with the personal economic interest of directors, commissioners, or substantial shareholders of the issuers or public companies (owning at least 20% shares of the issuer or public companies, either directly or indirectly), which may cause loss to the respective issuer or public company (BAPEPAM & LK Rule No. IX.E.1 on Affiliated Transaction and Conflict of Interest Transaction, Decree of the Head of BAPEPAM & LK No. KEP-412/BL/2009).
(3) OJK can obligate issuers or public companies to make certain announcement to the public no later than two working days after the date of transaction in the case of an 'Affiliated Transaction', which is a transaction that is entered into by and between an issuer or public company with its affiliate(s).
(4) The requirements and procedures for the granting of pre-emptive right, and transaction with conflict of interest and affiliated transaction, as referred to above are further stipulated by OJK.

[229] OJK Regulation No. 9/POJK.04/2018 defines 'Controlling Party' as a party owning 50% of shares or more, directly or indirectly, or a party with the ability to determine in any way, either directly or indirectly, the management and/or policy of the company.

[230] A party that fulfils this classification is considered the new Controlling Party and must conduct the tender offer for the remaining shares of the company, except for the following shares:

(1) the shares owned by shareholders who have entered into the acquisition transaction with the new Controlling Party;
(2) the shares owned by another party that has obtained an offer with the same terms and conditions from the new Controlling Party;
(3) the shares owned by another party, which at the same time conducts a tender offer over the same shares of the issuer;
(4) the shares owned by substantial shareholders; and
(5) the shares owned by another Controlling Party of the issuer.

[231] Contrary to the above, Article 27 of OJK Regulation No. 9/POJK.04/2018 provides exemption for the requirement to conduct a tender offer, where it will not be required for acquisition of a public company that is made indirectly through another public company, provided that the income contribution of the public company (in such other public company that is acquired) is less than 50% at the time the acquisition takes place pursuant to the consolidated financial report of such other public company.

[232] The tender offer must be initiated no later than the second working day after the acquisition takes place, which is deemed to have commenced from the submission of tender offer report to OJK. Further the tender offer must commence no later than six months after the date such announcements are made (announcement of takeover, announcement of negotiation, announcement of information, or transparency of information).

[233] Based on OJK Regulation No. 9/POJK.04/2018, in the case in which the implementation of a tender offer causes the share ownership of a new Controlling Party to exceed 80% of the paid up capital of the company, the new Controlling Party must re-transfer the shares to the public so that the shares owned by the public are at least 20% of the paid up capital of the company and must be commenced within a period of two years from the completion of the tender offer.

[234] Pursuant to OJK Regulation No. 9/POJK.04/2018, this regulation no longer gives a possibility to extend the period of reflotations of shares as previously allowed for a six-months extension period. The two-years period for the reflotation of shares is final and cannot be extended any further.

[235] Pursuant to OJK Regulation No. 54/POJK.04/2015 on Voluntary Tender Offer, a party that is willing to conduct a voluntary tender offer should submit a statement on the offer to OJK, and copy it to: (i) the stock exchange where the securities are listed; (ii) the target company; and (iii) any other party who has submitted a Voluntary Tender Offer announcement on Equity Securities of the same target company which offer period has not expired.

[236] The statement should be published in at least two Indonesian daily newspapers, where it is mandatory that one of the newspapers is circulated on a national level. After the publication, the offer cannot be annulled, unless OJK approves the annulment. The voluntary tender offer should start two days after the offer is effective. The offer will be held for thirty days and could be extended for ninety days with approval from OJK. The result of the offer should be reported to OJK, no later than ten days after the offer ends.

[237] Any party offering tender bids to purchase the stocks of issuers or public companies shall observe the provisions concerning transparency, propriety, and reporting as stipulated by OJK.

[238] The principle of transparency is the general guideline requiring issuers, public companies, and other parties subject to the Capital Market Law to inform the public at the latest two working days after the information or material fact is available of all material facts regarding their business condition or stocks that may affect the decision of investors on the said stocks and/or process of said stocks. To protect the interests of independent shareholders, generally being minority shareholders, from the possibility of improper price determination in transactions conducted by issuers resulting from the presence of conflict of interests with executive directors, commissioners, or substantial shareholders, OJK can require the issuer to obtain prior majority approval from its independent shareholders.

Statement of Independent Shareholders

[239] Before a GMS, the company must make available statement forms with adequate duty stamps to be signed by independent shareholders confirming that the parties concerned are truly independent shareholders. If later the statement turns out to be untrue, the relevant parties may be subject to a sanction based on the existing law.

[240] Issuers whose listing statements have become effective or public companies are obligated:

(a) to submit periodical reports to OJK and announce the reports to the public; and
(b) to submit reports to OJK on, and announce to the public, material events which may affect stock prices not later than the end of the second working day after such events.

[241] Issuers or public companies whose listing statements have become effective can be excepted from the obligation to submit the independent shareholder reports as referred to above on the basis of provisions laid down by OJK.

[242] Directors or commissioners of issuers or stock companies have to report to OJK their ownership and any change in their ownership of the corporate shares.

[243] Any party owning at least 5% of the shares of issuers or public companies must report to OJK their ownership and any change in their ownership of the corporate shares.

[244] The reports mentioned above must be submitted not later than ten days starting from the moment the ownership or change in ownership of the shares of issuers or public companies takes place.

[245] Specific provisions on and procedures for the submission of reports as mentioned above may be further stipulated by OJK.

[246] The information which must be submitted by the relevant parties to OJK based on the provisions in this law and/or its implementation rules must be made available to the public.

[247] Pursuant to BAPEPAM & LK Rule IX.E.1 on Transaction with Affiliated Parties and Conflict of Interest on Certain Transaction, Decree of the Head of BAPEPAM & LK No. Kep-412/BL/2009, exceptions to obtaining prior approval from independent shareholders in the case of a conflict of interest transaction can be made by OJK under the following circumstances:

(1) the use of each facility given by the company or a controlled company to members of the board of commissioners, members of the board of directors, and/or substantial shareholders in their capacity as employees and the facility is directly related to their responsibilities to the company is in conformity with the company's policy, which has been approved at a GMS;
(2) transaction between the company and its employees, members of directors, or members of commissioners of the company or between the company and the employees, members of directors, or members of commissioners of a controlled company, or between the controlled company and employees, directors, or commissioners of the controlled company or between the controlled company and the employees, directors, or commissioners of the company under the same requirements, as long as the transaction has been approved by the GMS. The transaction also covers the benefit given by the company or the controlled company to all employees, directors, or commissioners on the same terms in accordance with the company's policy;
(3) remuneration, including salaries, pension fund contribution, and/or special benefits given to commissioners, directors, and substantial shareholders, which are also in their capacity as employees, if the total remuneration is disclosed in the periodic financial statement;
(4) the ongoing transactions conducted after the company made a Public Offering or after the registration statement becomes effective as a public company, with the following requirements:
    (a) the first transaction that underlay the ongoing transactions has already met the rules under the regulations;
    (b) the terms and conditions of the transactions are not detrimental to the company.
(5) transaction not exceeding 0.5% in value of the paid-up capital and does not exceed IDR5 000 000 000;
(6) transaction conducted by the company as implementation of prevailing regulations or court decision; and/or
(7) a transaction between a company and a controlled company whose shares or capital are at least 99% held by the company or transaction between two controlled companies, whose shares or capital are at least 99% owned by the holding company.

Other Relevant Laws and Due Diligence Issues

[248] The anti-corruption laws may affect M&A activity, as regulated under the Law Number 31 of 1999 as amended by Law Number 20 of 2001 on Eradication of Criminal Acts of Corruption. However, the anti-bribery or anti-corruption laws have not been rigorously enforced in the Capital Market due to limited competence of the investigators. Therefore, the OJK through OJK Regulations No. 29/POJK.04/2016 on submission of annual reports of the listed company or public company requires the corporation to have a transparency system, including a whistleblower system, where the corporations may report on the violations.

[249] The US Foreign Corrupt Practices Act (FCPA) and the UK Bribery Act may have the effect on M&A activity in Indonesia, in terms of the companies who perform M&A activity originate from USA and UK or have a presence there.

[250] Recently, the bribery and corruption practice are improving due to the actions of the Corruption Eradication Commission (*KPK*) to eradicate the corruption practice in Indonesia.

[251] The money-laundering regulations consist of:

(a) Law No. 8/2010 on the Criminal Acts of Money Laundering.
(b) Presidential Regulation No. 50/2011 on the Implementation Procedure on the Authority of the Central Reporting and Financial Transaction Analysis.
(c) OJK Regulation No. 12/POJK.01/2017 on Implementation of Program of Anti Money Laundering and Prevention of Terrorism Funding in Financial Service Sector.

In this regulation, the principle of know your customer is the pre-emptive action against the money-laundering crime. The implementation of this principle starts from the customer that is going to conduct an investment in the Capital Market through the mechanism of receiving and identifying the customer. Under this mechanism, a financial services provider shall request the information on the background, and identity of the prospective customer, the objective and purpose of the account opening and other information that might enable to obtain the profile of the prospective customer.

[252] There are significant environmental or product safeties laws will need to be considered, which are:

(a) Law Number 32 of 2009 on the Environmental Protection and Management.
(b) Government Regulation Number 27 of 2012 on the Environmental License.
(c) Minister of Environmental Regulation Number 5/2012 on the Types of Business Plan and/or Activities that Shall Has Environmental Impact Analysis.

[253] Since Indonesia became the member of the World Trade Organization by ratifying the *General Agreement on Tariffs and Trade (GATT)*, the Indonesian regulation on IPR has been enhanced. As the consequence, the Indonesian Government has enacted legislation dealing with IPR. The legal protection under the law consists of several elements, which are:

(a) Subject of protection
The subject that is concerned is the owner or the holder of the rights.
(b) Object of protection
The object that is concerned is the every types of regulated IPR under the laws, which are copyright, trade mark, trade secrets, patent, etc.
(c) Registration of the protection
The IPR that are protected are only those that are registered and evidenced with the certificate of registration, except where the laws regulate otherwise, such as copyrights that cannot be registered under the Law Number 28 of 2014 on Copyright.
(d) Period of protection
The concerned period is for how long the IPR is protected by the Laws, such as the trademark for period of ten years and may be extended again, patent for period of twenty years and may be extended again, etc.
(e) Legal action of protection
If there is a violation on the IPR, therefore the offender shall be punished, both through civil action and criminal action.

[254] Therefore, the registration, protection and enforcement of the IPR have been accommodated by the establishment of the legislation on IPR. Due to the Legal Due Diligence process, the IPR may be audited through the certificate that used as proof and checked through the registration office of the concerned IPR.

[255] There is no any mandatory compensation on termination of the distributor agreements if the termination complies with the reasons that set out under the Article 22 of the Minister of Trade Regulation No. 11/M-DAG/PER/3/2006, which are:

(a) Termination based on the mutual consent of both parties.
(b) Unilateral termination, if:
   (i) The company is liquidated.
   (ii) The company dismisses his business activities.
   (iii) If the distributor/agent rights is transferred to another party.
   (iv) If the company is bankrupt.
   (v) The agreement is not extended.

[256] In addition, for the unilateral termination by the principal, and the principal is going to appoint the new distributor/agent before the registration letter/*surat tanda pendaftaran* (STP) is expired, there should be a clean break between the principal and the former agent/distributor (in form of written mutual consent that states that the commitment between the parties is finished).

[257] The issues with the valuation of intangible assets (IPR) are on the expiration date of the certificate of rights, the registration of the rights with respect to whether it has been registered by others and in terms of the trademark if the license holders on the trademark are not well recorded. The valuation issue that may frequently arise is the dispute between both parties claiming that they are the one who is entitled to particular IPR instead of others.

[258] In terms of the target company being bound during the acquisition process, there is a possibility of clauses dealing with 'change of control' in agreements. Specifically in bank loan arrangements, the clause may be included in order to provide legal certainty for the repayment to the bank. These are pursuant to Article 1338 of the ICC which sets out the principle of freedom of contact.

The Due Diligence Process

[259] As the consequence of the process of merger and acquisition, the acquiring company and the acquired company will agree under the Memorandum of Understanding between the parties and will enter into an agreement for the confidentiality of the information that is obtained from the full due diligence. Then, concerning with property, the part of due diligence process will obligate the target company to provide the required documents evidencing ownership of property. Commonly, the due diligence will also use 'data rooms' of the target company to obtain the required documents.

[260] Legislative issues that may be considered critical to the process of due diligence is the amendment of laws and regulations that are related with the business activities of company. This particular issue may complicate the process of due diligence of the company, if the company has not adjusted with the changes that are required under the applicable laws and regulations. An example of this particular issue is the revision of the Negative Investment List. If the Negative Investment List is amended, while the company is in the process of due diligence, this may complicate the process and may extend the time of due diligence. In relation to this issue and the location of the company, the Negative Investment List's provisions may be differenced based on the location where the company performs its business activities.

[261] A problem arising in the context of due diligence and planning is miscalculation of the financial statements of the target company. This particular issue may lead to losses for the company in case there is an excess of receivables that will be claimed by a third party.

[262] An example of due-diligence problems is the *ABNR law firm v. Sumatra LLC case*. The alleged due diligence issues being:

(a) On the review of the fiduciary guarantee on twelve trucks
Sumatra LLC provided a loan in amount of USD2 million to PT Bangun Karya Pratama Lestari ('*BPKL*') to purchase trucks, which were guaranteed with a fiduciary security interest in the event of BKPL's default to repay the loan. However, in fact, when BKPL defaulted it emerged that the trucks have previously already been burdened with a fiduciary security interest to other parties.
(b) On the review of the bank guarantee held by the BKPL

Other than the double fiduciary guarantee, the bank guarantee used by the BKPL was allegedly false.

[263] The relationship between the formal due diligence and the imposition of the contractual representations, warranties, and indemnities is on the role of the formal due diligence as an action of confirmation of the agreed clauses of representations, warranties, and indemnities. Even though, the due diligence is not obligated under the laws and regulations. In practice, most of the acquisition processes always involve the due diligence process, because it provides certainty.

Role of the Courts

[264] Indonesian judicial system has three main principles, which are simple, fast, and cheap. However, in practice, the implementation of the judicial system is neither simple, nor fast or cheap because in fact, cases at the appellate levels are backlogged. Therefore, this situation may affect the amount it may cost the company to pay lawyers. In addition, the prevalence of corruption in the judicial system causes the mechanism itself to not work effectively.

[265] During the judicial proceeding, the judges have several factors that may affect their decision. One of the factors is the origin of the parties, therefore, if the dispute is between domestic residents or company and foreigners, the judges have a tendency to support the domestic residents or company over the foreigners, particularly at Courts of First Instance.

[266] Besides the court, there are several other alternative dispute resolution mechanisms, which are:

(a) Negotiation
In this mechanism, the parties may directly meet in order to jointly discuss the dispute in a cooperative and open manner.

(b) Mediation
The elements of mediation consist of: voluntary dispute settlement, intervention/assistance, impartial third party, decision-making by the parties based on consensus and active participation. In the mediation process, there is no coercion element between the parties and the mediator, because both of the parties voluntary request the mediator to assist the settlement of the conflict. Therefore, the mediator shall be impartial and also actively participate in the settlement process.

(c) Conciliation
Conciliation has similarities with mediation. Both of those mechanisms involve a third party to settle the dispute. However, for the conciliation, the conciliator is only acting as the facilitator in order to hold the meeting between the parties to resolve their own dispute.

(d) Arbitration
Arbitration is held based on a contract between the parties. In arbitration, the power to settle the dispute is in accordance with the discretion or amicable settlement of the arbitrators. Compared to the court settlement which

is open to the public, arbitration is not, and arbitration is performed with amicable settlement and both of the parties choose their own arbitrator that will be decide and rule the dispute.

[267] If a dispute is pursued through the courts, a civil case will take:

(a) District court: five months.
(b) High Court: three months.
(c) Supreme Court: 250 days.

In practice, it may take significantly more time than the aforementioned time frames.

MERGER CONTROLS. ANTITRUST/COMPETITION ISSUES

[268] In 2001, the new law on anti-monopolistic activities and unfair competition became effective. It is in essence Indonesia's antitrust law. The antitrust law provides that certain mergers and acquisitions must be approved in advance by the Commission (the supervising body entrusted by the law with breach of compliance and dispute settlement). The criteria for determining which mergers fall under the potential authority of the Business Competition Supervisory Commission (the '*Commission*' or '*KPPU*') is provided in Government Regulation Number 57 of 2010 on Merger or Consolidation of Business Entities and Acquisition of Company Shares that could result in Monopolistic Practices and/or Unfair Business Competition.

Mergers under Law No. 5/1999 on Prohibition of Monopolistic Practice and Unfair Business Competition

[269] Indonesia's 'new' antitrust law was promulgated in 1999 and has been in force since 5 March 2000. Despite its title, this refers to prohibition of 'monopolistic practices', this law contains provisions against 'engineered' market dominance and the control of activities by so-called business actors who already possess a dominant market position.

[270] Monopolistic practice is the concentration of economic power by one or more business actors, resulting in unhealthy business competition and potential harm to the public interest. Unfair business competition is competition between business actors in undertaking production activities and/or marketing of goods and/or services in a dishonest or illegal fashion or restructuring business competition.

[271] A 'dominant position' is defined as a situation in which a business actor has no significant competitor in the relevant market in relation to the market share controlled by that business actor or in which a business actor has the highest position among its competitors in the relevant market in relation to financial capacity, access to suppliers or sales, and the ability to influence supply and demand of certain goods or services. Finally, a 'business actor' is defined to be any individual or business entity either incorporated as legal entity, established and domiciled in or conducting activities in the jurisdiction of the Republic of Indonesia either individually or jointly based on an agreement, conducting various business activities in the economic sector.

[272] Article 16 of Law No. 5/1999 provides that business actors are prohibited from entering into agreements with other parties abroad that contain provisions that could result in the occurrence of monopolistic practices and unfair business competition. In connection with the definition of a business actor as set out above, this means that at least one party must be Indonesian, while the other is foreign. The application of the Indonesian antitrust law is therefore ruled out in relation to agreements where both parties are domiciled abroad and the effects of their agreement are evident in the Indonesian market. Article 16 of Law No. 5/1999 only covers 'agreements' and arguably does not cover compliance with statutory obligations as a result of an offshore merger or acquisition.

[273] Business actors are prohibited from conducting mergers or consolidations of business entities that could result in the occurrence of monopolistic practice and/or unfair business competition. A business actor is prohibited from conducting the acquisition of shares in other companies if such acquisition may result in the occurrence of monopolistic practices and/or unfair business competition.

[274] The Law No. 5/1999 provides that merger or consolidation of business entities or acquisition of shares which result in the value of the assets and/or the value of the sales exceeding a certain amount must be reported to the Commission no later than thirty days after the date on which the said merger, consolidation or acquisition took place.

[275] One indication of the Commission's authority with regard to mergers is Article 35 of Law No. 5/1999 on duties of the Commission. The duties of the Commission are to conduct evaluations as to whether there is any abuse of dominant position that could result in the occurrence of monopolistic practices and/or unfair business competition as referred to in Articles 25–28 of Law No. 5/1999. Article 28 of Law No. 5/1999 deals with proposed mergers and acquisitions and does not deal with concluded mergers to be reported under Article 29 of Law No. 5/1999. The authorities of the Commission include investigation, summoning, and imposing administrative sanctions in the form of cancelling mergers and acquisitions of shares as referred to in Article 28 of Law No. 5/1999.

[276] Of note in the Indonesian Antitrust Act are its criminal sanctions. Violations of the provisions in Article 28 of Law No. 5/1999 are subject to a criminal fine of at least IDR25 billion and not more than IDR100 billion or imprisonment in lieu of a fine for a maximum of six months. Additional criminal penalties can take the form of: revocation of the business permit, a prohibition on holding a position as director for at least two years up to a maximum of five years, or cessation of certain activities that have caused losses to third parties.

[277] In accordance with Article 29 of Law No. 5/1999 and Article 5 paragraph (1) of Government Regulation Number 57 of 2010 on Merger or Consolidation of Business Entities and the Acquisition of Shares That Can Cause Monopolistic Practices and Unfair Business Competition ('*GR No. 57/2010*'), the method of evaluation is an evaluation after the merger or consolidation occurs (*post-evaluation*). This means that after the business actors conduct a merger, consolidation or acquisition of shares, the surviving company has to notify the KPPU. Such notification has to be submitted by completing a form contained in KPPU Regulation No. 10 of 2010 on Notification Form of Merger, Consolidation and Acquisition of a Company's Shares. Pursuant to Article 29 of Law No. 5/1999 and Article 5 of GR No. 57/2010, notification of merger or consolidation has to be made to the KPPU no later than thirty working days from the date that such merger, consolidation or acquisition is legally effective. Violations of the provisions in Article 29 of Law No. 5/1999 are subject to an administrative fine of IDR1 billion for each day of delay, for a total of not more than IDR25 billion.

[278] Nevertheless, Article 10 of GR No. 57/2010 also provides a right for the business actor to consult the KPPU voluntarily, either in written or verbal form prior to performing the merger, consolidation or acquisition. This consultation is governed under KPPU Regulation No. 11 of 2010 on Consultation of Merger or Consolidation of Business Entities and Acquisition of a Company's Shares.

[279] As such, based on Article 29 of Law No. 5/1999, and Articles 5 and 10 of GR No. 57/2010, there are two types of evaluation of merger, consolidation, and acquisition that are performed by the KPPU: (a) Post-evaluation (Notification), which is mandatory; and (b) Pre-evaluation (Consultation), which is voluntary. The evaluation can be conducted personally/proactively by the business actors with the relevant authorities. However, experience in such matters is typically required, either internally or through outside advisors.

Pre-evaluation

[280] Pre-Evaluations are not binding upon the Commission and do not exempt parties from the Post-Evaluation notification requirements. However, according to KPPU Regulation No. 13 of 2010, as amended by KPPU Regulation No. 10 of 2011, and as amended for the second time by KPPU Regulation No. 3 of 2012, and as lastly amended for the third time by KPPU Regulation No. 2 of 2013, on the Guidelines of Merger or Consolidation of Business Entities and Acquisition of a Company's Shares That Can Cause Monopolistic Practices and Unfair Business Competition, the regulator will not proceed to re-assess a transaction for which parties have obtained pre-closing guidance, unless there have been material changes in the transaction structure or the market conditions.

[281] Under the Pre-Evaluation/consultation process, the Commission is required to complete a preliminary review within thirty days of the acceptance of the Pre-Evaluation/consultation submission. If potential anti-competitive effects are identified, the Commission can either issue a letter of objection or a letter of no objection with restrictive conditions attached, or, if it considers further examination is necessary, initiate a further review that may last for an additional sixty days.

[282] The Commission evaluates the merger, consolidation or acquisition transaction based on five aspects, which are as follows: market concentration, entry barriers, anti-competition potential, efficiency, and bankruptcy. These five aspects will be thoroughly analysed by the Commission and will result in one of the three possible assessments:

(a) There is no potential of monopoly or unfair business practices.
(b) There is potential of monopoly or unfair business practices.
(c) There is no potential of monopoly or unfair business practices. However, business must follow several suggestions from the Commission to prevent monopoly and unfair business practices (opinion with remedy).

Post-evaluation

[283] As mentioned above, within thirty days of the effective date of such transaction, notification of merger, consolidation or acquisition has to be made to the KPPU. Once the notification is complete, the Commission has a maximum of ninety working days to review the transaction. Commission will issue the Commission's Opinion towards the results of such transaction. Output of the assessment notification will be same as in the Pre-Evaluation stages in that are (i) there is no potential; (ii) there is potential, and (iii) there is no potential but with remedy for monopoly and unfair business practices.

[284] Under KPPU Regulation No. 13 of 2010, as amended lastly by KPPU Regulation No. 2 of 2013, it has been determined that the business actors are required to notify the merger, consolidation or acquisition to the KPPU if it meets the value thresholds and is not a merger, consolidation, or acquisition between affiliated companies.

Value Thresholds

[285]

(1) Asset value of the business entity resulting from the merger, consolidation or acquisition exceeds IDR2 500 000 000 000.00.
(2) Revenue of the business entity resulting from the merger, consolidation or acquisition exceeds IDR5 000 000 000 000.00.

(3) For the banking sector, where asset value of the business entity resulting from the merger, consolidation or acquisition exceeds IDR20 000 000 000 000.00.

Affiliated Companies

[286] Based on the elucidation of Article 7 of GR No. 57/2010, 'affiliated' companies are defined as where:

(1) one company, either directly or indirectly, controls or is controlled by the other company;
(2) the companies are controlled, either directly or indirectly, by the same parties; or
(3) there is a relationship between the companies and the main shareholder.

[287] Up until September 2018, there have not been any business actors that have conducted a Pre-Evaluation and/or Post-Evaluation and have been considered to have a potential of a monopoly or an unfair business practice.

TAXATION ASPECTS

[288] A company is treated as a resident of Indonesia for tax purposes by virtue of having its incorporation or its domicile is in Indonesia. A foreign company carrying out business activities through a permanent establishment ('*PE*') in Indonesia will generally have to assume the same tax obligations as a resident taxpayer.

[289] Tax subject is categorized into two groups; those are resident tax subject and non-resident tax subject.

[290] Parties who are considered as a resident tax subject are:

- an individual who resides in Indonesia;
- an individual who is present in Indonesia more than 183 days in any twelve-month period;
- an individual who is present in Indonesia during a tax year and intends to reside in Indonesia;
- a statutory body that is established or domiciled in Indonesia.

[291] Parties who are considered as a non-resident tax subject are:

- an individual who does not reside in Indonesia, but he/she receives or earns income from Indonesia;
- an individual who is present in Indonesia for no more than 183 days in any twelve-month period, but he/she receives or earns income from Indonesia;
- a statutory body that is not established or domiciled in Indonesia, but carries on business through a permanent establishment in Indonesia or receives or

earns income from Indonesia not resulting from carrying on business in Indonesia.

[292] A PE is considered a non-resident tax subject.

[293] Indonesian PEs of foreign companies have to settle their tax liabilities either by direct payments, third party withholdings, or a combination of both.

[294] Article 25 of Income Tax Law, the monthly tax instalments constitute the first part of tax payments to be made by resident taxpayers and Indonesian PEs as a prepayment of their current year Corporate Income Tax ('*CIT*') liability. A monthly tax instalment is generally calculated using the most recent corporate tax return. Special instalment calculations apply for new taxpayers, finance lease companies, banks, state-owned companies, listed companies and other taxpayer with periodical reporting requirements.

[295] Article 23 of Income Tax Law, the tax withheld by third parties on certain income or tax to be paid in advance on certain transactions (e.g., Article 22 of Income Tax Law on imports) also constitute prepayments for the current year CIT liability of the income recipient or the party conducting the import.

[296] Articles 22, 23, and 25 of Income Tax Law, if the total amounts of tax paid in advance through the year, and Article 24 of Income Tax Law for the tax paid abroad are less than the total CIT due, the company concerned has to settle the shortfall before filing its Corporate Income Tax Return (CITR). Such payment is referred to as Article 29 of Income Tax Law.

[297] Certain types of income earned by resident taxpayers or Indonesian PEs are subject to final income tax. In this respect, the tax withheld by third parties (referred to as Article 4 paragraph (2) of Income Tax Law) constitutes the final settlement of the income tax for that particular income.

[298] In addition, for foreign companies without PE(s) in Indonesia, the tax withheld from their Indonesia-sourced income by the Indonesian party paying the income (Article 26 of Income Tax Law) constitutes a final settlement of their income tax due.

[299] Generally, a flat rate of 25% corporate income tax will apply. Public companies that satisfy a minimum listing requirement of 40% and other conditions are entitled to a tax discount off the standard rate, giving them an effective tax rate of 20%. Small enterprises, i.e., corporate taxpayers with an annual turnover of not more than IDR50 billion, are entitled to a 50% discount of the standard tax rate which is imposed proportionally on taxable income of the part of gross turnover up to IDR4.8 billion. For taxpayers with annual gross turnover of not more than IDR4.8 billion, the final tax rate is 0.5%

[300] Generally, capital gains derived from the sale of Indonesian assets held by foreigners are taxable at a rate of 5% of the gross proceeds (20% of estimated net income of 25% of the sale price). Non-resident taxpayers may be protected from tax by the provision of any applicable tax treaties.

[301] Listed shares sold on the exchange by non-resident and resident tax payers are subject to a withholding tax of 0.1% of the transaction value. Founder shares also are subject to an additional final tax of 0.5% of the share value at prescribed times.

[302] The VAT rate generally is 10%. This may be increased or decreased to 15% or 5% according to a government regulation. Certain goods and services are exempt. Exports of taxable goods, intangibles, and certain taxable services are zero rated.

[303] Stamp duty applies to letters of agreements, notarial deeds, deeds prepared by a designated land notary, all documents bearing a sum of money, and documents to be used as instruments of evidence before a court. The rates are nominal, ranging from IDR3 000 and IDR6 000, depending on the amount of the transaction and type of document.

[304] Land and building tax (Real Estate Tax) is payable annually on land, buildings and permanent structures. The rate is depend on the regional government regulation, typically not more than 0.3% of the value of the property, although higher rates apply to a certain high-value housing and large estates.

[305] A land and building acquisition duty of 5% is payable when a person obtains right to land or a building with a value greater than IDR60 million. Various exemptions apply, including on transfers in connection with a merger and transfers to relatives.

[306] Employers are required to withhold Article 21 or 26 of Income Tax Law on a monthly basis from the salaries and other compensation payable to their employees. If an employee is a resident taxpayer, the amount of tax withheld should be based on the normal tax rates. If the employee is a non-resident taxpayer, the withholding tax is 20% of the gross amount (and may be set at a lower rate under a tax treaty).

[307] According to Article 16 of Presidential Regulation No. 19 of 2016 on Second Amendment on Presidential Regulation No. 12 of 2013 on Health Security (*Jaminan Kesehatan*), for healthcare coverage through BPJS *Kesehatan*, the employer contributes 4% and the employee contributes 1%. In addition, according to Government Regulation Number 84 of 2013 on Ninth Amendment of Government Regulation Number 14 of 1993 on Implementation of the Program of Worker's Social Security for retirement scheme (*Jaminan Hari Tua*) 3.7% of wages (from employer) and 2% (from employee).

[308] Any goods coming from overseas into Indonesian customs area generally are subject to import duty and import taxes. Certain exemptions apply (e.g., goods in a bonded zone or warehouse and goods in an import facility for export purposes).

[309] Excise duties are also imposed on certain goods as part of the government's effort to control the distribution of such goods in Indonesia (e.g., alcohol and tobacco products).

[310] In relation to the tax incentive for takeovers, mergers and acquisitions, assets may be transferred at book value as part of a merger or in the context of certain other reorganizations, subject to prior approval from the Director General of Taxation. The transfer of titles to land and buildings under an asset purchased subjects the seller to a 2.5% final income tax and subjects the acquirer to a 5% transfer of title tax (duty). In addition, under an approved merger, consolidation, and expansion there may be partial (50 percent) relief from the 5% transfer of title tax and full relief from the 2,5% income tax on land and buildings.

[311] With respect to thin capitalization, Indonesia does not have specific thin capitalization rules, but the general law authorizes the Ministry of Finance to determine the debt-to-equity ratio of companies for tax calculation purposes.

[312] Indonesia's Director General of Taxation has issued Regulation No. 25/PJ/2017 on Implementation of Determination of Amount of Company's Debt To Equity Ratio For Purpose of Calculating Income Tax And Procedure For Reporting Foreign Private Debt, providing implementing regulations on Indonesia's thin capitalization rules by applying a 4:1 debt-to-equity ratio ('*DER*'), and includes an obligation to report the DER calculation and private overseas loan details to the Director General of Taxation as part of the company's income tax return.

[313] Transfer Pricing in the Context of Article 18 paragraph (3) of Income Tax Law allows the Directorate General of Taxation to, after the fact, reallocate income and debt of taxpayers in a special relationship. The taxable income can be recalculated using the price comparison method between independent parties, the resale price method, the cost-plus method, as well as other methods.

[314] A special relationship is deemed to exist, under Article 18 paragraph (4) of Income Tax Law, if:

(a) Taxpayer has capital participation directly or indirectly at least 25% upon another Taxpayers; the relationship between Taxpayers through ownership at least 25% upon two or more Taxpayers; or relationship between two or more Taxpayers mentioned late.
(b) Taxpayer controls the other Taxpayer or two or more Taxpayers are under the same control, either directly or indirectly; or
(c) There are family relationship either blood relationship or by marriage in vertical and/or horizontal lineage of one degree.

[315] In addition, the Directorate General of Tax issued Regulation No. PER 22/PJ/2013 on Tax Audit Procedures for Taxpayers with Related Party Transactions.

[316] The revenue authorities have issued special regulations with respect to mergers and acquisitions, including income tax aspects, the treatment of losses, etc. To a certain extent these regulations are not synchronized with the legal aspects or the accounting treatment of this kind of transaction, especially with respect to mergers. Indonesian tax laws tend to view mergers of any kind for taxation purposes as acquisitions of assets.

[317] On 17 July 2007, the Government promulgated Law No. 28/2007 on Third Amendment on Law No. 6/1983 on General Provisions and Procedures of Taxation, which became effective on 1 January 2008, which lastly amended again with Law No. 16/2009 containing a minor change. The Law No. 28/2007 has a considerable focus on improvements of the tax assessment system and filing procedures of tax returns *(Surat Pemberitahuan Pajak);* provisions on income tax are currently regulated by Law No. 36/2008 on the 4th Amendment of Law No. 7/1983 on Income Tax.

Law No. 7/1983 on Income Tax, as Already Amended by Law No. 7/1991, Law No. 10/1994, Law No. 17/2000, and Law No. 36/2008 ('*Income Tax Law*')

[318] All forms of income are subject to tax, including any economic benefit received or earned by the taxpayer from within as well as outside Indonesia, which can be used for consumption or to increase the wealth of the taxpayer concerned, in whatever names and forms, including:

(a) compensation or rewards received or earned in connection with work or services, covering salaries, wages, allowances, honorariums, commissions, bonuses, gratuities, pensions, or other forms of recompense except otherwise stipulated by this law;
(b) prizes from lotteries or work or activities, and awards;
(c) profits from business;
(d) gains from the sale or transfer of property, including:
  (i) gains due to the transfer of property to a corporation, partnership, and other organizations in lien of shares or capital participation;
  (ii) gains accruing to a corporation, partnership, or other organization due to the transfer of property to shareholders, partners or members;
  (iii) gains due to liquidation, merger, fusion, expansion, division, or takeover of business;
  (iv) gains due to the transfer of wealth in the form of a grant, aid or a contribution, except that given to a direct blood relative, and a religious organization, educational organization, a social organization or a small-scale business unit or a cooperative as stipulated by the Minister of Finance, as long as it has nothing to do with business, work, ownership or control between the parties concerned.
(e) refunds of tax payments already calculated as a cost;
(f) interest including premiums, discounts, and recompense due to a debt repayment guarantee;
(g) dividends, in whatever names and forms, including dividends paid by an insurance company to policyholders, and payments of business profits of a cooperative;
(h) royalties;
(i) rents and other income connected with the use of property;

(j) annuities received or accruing;
(k) gains due to cancellation of debts;
(l) gains due to a foreign currency exchange rate difference;
(m) a surplus due to revaluation of assets;
(n) insurance premiums;
(o) contributions received or accruing to an association from its members viz. a taxpayer engaged in business or independent work as long as the contributions are determined on the basis of the volume of business or independent work of its members;
(p) an increase in net assets from income not yet subject to tax;
(q) income from sharia business;
(r) compensation as stipulated by Laws concerning General Provisions and Tax Procedures; and
(s) surplus of Bank Indonesia.

[319] Taxable income for the resident taxpayer and permanently established shall be determined on the basis of gross income after deducting:

(a) costs of earning, recovering, and securing such income, including costs of buying materials, costs connected with work or services viz. wages, salaries, honorariums, bonuses, gratuities, and allowances in the form of money, interest, rents, royalties, travel expenses, waste processing costs, bad claims, insurance premiums, administration costs, and taxes except income tax;
(b) depreciation of expenditure to obtain tangible business property and amortization of expenditure to obtain rights and other costs with a useful life of more than one year;
(c) contributions to a pension fund approved by the Minister of Finance;
(d) losses due to the sale or transfer of property owned and used in business or owned to earn, recover and secure income;
(e) losses due to a foreign currency exchange rate difference;
(f) costs of corporate research and development conducted in Indonesia;
(g) costs of scholarships, apprenticeships, and training;
(h) receivables which cannot be claimed, subject to following conditions:
    (i) it has been charged as an expense in the commercial profit/loss report;
    (ii) the relevant taxpayer must submit a list of receivables which cannot be claimed to the Directorate General of Taxation;
    (iii) the settlement has been transferred to the district court or the State Agency for Receivable Settlement and Auction, or there is a written agreement for write-off between the respective parties; it has been published in a public or special publication; or there is creditor's which states certain amount of bad debts have been written off;
    (iv) the requirement stated in number (iii) does not apply for small debtors.
(i) donation for national disaster which is stipulated by a Government Regulation;
(j) donation for research and development conducted in Indonesia which is stipulated by a Government Regulation;

(k) costs of social infrastructure development which is stipulated by a Government Regulation;
(l) donation in the form of education facilities which is stipulated by a Government Regulation;
(m) donation for sport enhancement which is stipulated by a Government Regulation.

[320] If the gross income after deductions registers a loss, the loss may be offset against income arising in the next year for five successive years.

[321] The acquisition value or transfer value of property transferred within the framework of a liquidation, merger, fusion, expansion, division, or takeover of business will equal the amount which should be spent or received on the basis of the market price, unless otherwise stipulated by the Minister of Finance.

Minister of Finance Regulation No. 52/PMK.010/2017 on the Use of Book Value on the Transfer of Assets for Business Merger, Consolidation, Expansion, or Acquisition

[322] Corporate taxpayers are allowed to use book values on the transfer of assets in the context of business mergers, consolidations expansions, or acquisitions upon approval from the Directorate General of Taxation, and shall meet the following requirements:

(i) The application is filed within six months after the effective date of the business transaction by attaching the reason and purpose of the business transactions;
(ii) Fulfilling the business purpose test; and
(iii) Obtaining a tax clearance letter (*Surat Keterangan Fiskal*) for each of the relevant domestic corporate taxpayers or PE.

[323] Business purpose tests are fulfilled if, among others, assets that are approved to be transferred using book value cannot be transferred to another party within two years after the effective date of the business transaction, except if it is carried out as part of increasing the company's efficiency.

[324] In the case of the mergers, consolidations, or acquisitions of a business being executed in the current tax year, the amount of instalment of Income Tax Article 25 from the parties who receive assets, the transfer may not be less than the amount of instalment of Income Tax Article 25 from all relevant taxpayers prior to the mergers, consolidations, or acquisitions. Settlement of income tax for the current tax year through payment, deduction and / or collection of income tax prior to the merger, consolidation, expansion, or acquisition of business from domestic corporate taxpayers and permanent establishments who transfer property, can be transferred into current year income tax payments from Taxpayers who receive transfers.

Minister of Finance Regulation No. 79/PMK.03/2008 on Revaluation of Corporate Fixed Assets for Taxation Purpose jo. the Director General of Taxation Regulation No. 12/PJ/2009 on the Procedures and Administration of Applications for Revaluation of Corporate Fixed Assets for the Purposes of Taxation

[325] Revaluation of fixed assets may be conducted by any company as long as they are a resident corporate taxpayer and PE, excluding companies holding a license to perform bookkeeping in English and US Dollars, which is subject to approval of Director General of Taxation. The revaluation of fixed assets must be calculated/ conducted on the basis of the market value or the proper value obtained at the time the revaluation is conducted using the revaluation method normally prevailing in Indonesia, which is stipulated by appraisal service providers or appraisers holding a license from the government.

[326] In the event that the market value or the proper value determined by the appraising company or the appraiser recognized by the government turns out not to reflect the actual condition, the Director General of Taxation may, in the context of tax calculation, adjust the market value or the proper value of the assets concerned.

[327] The difference between the transfer value of corporate fixed assets and the remaining fiscal book value upon the transfer shall constitute profit or loss on the basis of the Income Tax Law.

[328] In the event that a taxpayer transfers corporate fixed assets in the framework of a business merger which secures approval it is not subject to the Article 8 paragraph (1) of Regulation of Minister of Finance No. 79/PMK.03/2008 where for a certain fixed asset of groups 1, 2, 3, and 4 the positive difference of revaluation above the previous remaining book value shall be subject to additional final income tax at a rate equal to the highest rate of income tax on resident taxpayers effective upon the revaluation.

[329] Any surplus in the revaluation of fixed assets after an offset for a loss has been given shall be subject to the imposition of a final 10% income tax. In the case the company cannot settle the income tax due to financial condition thereof it may submit an application for paying the tax by instalments maximally over twelve months.

Law No. 42/2009 on the Third Amendment of Law No. 8/1983 on Value Added Tax on Goods and Services and Sales Tax on Luxury Goods

[330] The customs area is the territory of the Republic of Indonesia in which customs laws are effective.

[331] Goods are tangible goods which by nature or law can take the form of movable or immovable goods as well as intangible items.

[332] Taxable goods shall be goods as defined below which are subject to tax on the basis of this law. Luxury Goods Sales Tax (LGST) rates range from 10% and maximum 200%.

[333] The following come within the definition of the delivery of taxable goods:

(a) the delivery of rights to taxable goods pursuant to an agreement;
(b) the transfer of taxable goods pursuant to a hire purchase agreement or a leasing agreement;
(c) the delivery of taxable goods to an intermediary or through an auctioneer;
(d) for own use and transferred free of charge;
(e) an inventory of taxable goods and assets originally not part of the transaction which is left over upon the dissolution of a company, as long as the value added tax on the acquisition of such assets is creditable pursuant to relevant provisions;
(f) the delivery of taxable goods from the head office to branches or vice versa and the delivery of taxable goods between branches;
(g) the delivery of taxable goods on consignment;
(h) the delivery of Taxable Goods by a Taxable Entrepreneur in the context of a financing agreement conducted on the basis of shariah principles, which delivery is considered to be directly from the Taxable Entrepreneur to the party that needs the Taxable Goods.

The following are excluded from the definition of the delivery of taxable goods:

(a) the delivery of taxable goods to a broker as referred to in the Commercial Code;
(b) the delivery of taxable goods as collateral for a loan;
(c) the delivery of taxable goods from the head office to branches or vice versa and the delivery of taxable goods between branches, in the event the taxable entrepreneur has obtained permit for centralization tax due *(Ijin Pemusatan Pajak Terutang)* pursuant to prevailing regulations;
(d) the transfer of Taxable Goods in the context of a business merger, consolidation, expansion, split, or takeover provided that the party making the transfer and the party receiving the transfer are Taxable Entrepreneurs; and
(e) Taxable Goods in the form of assets that were not originally intended to be traded, which remain at the time a company is dissolved, and the Input Tax on whose acquisition was not creditable.

EMPLOYMENT CONSIDERATIONS

[334] Article 163 paragraph (1) of Law No. 13/2003 provides that employees should have a choice to refuse or accept which employer they work for, in the event of the change in status of the company through a merger, consolidation or acquisition. Under Article 163 paragraph (2) of the Law No. 13/2003, in the event of change in status, merger, or consolidation, the employer has the right to refuse the employees.

[335] There is no requirement that employees be entitled to management representation on either the board of directors or the board of commissioners. Management representation is regulated by Law No. 40/2007. In addition, a company's articles of association can provide a procedure and requirements relating to the management representation.

[336] According to Article 127 paragraphs (1) and (2) of Law No. 40/2007, an employer whose company is engaging in a merger or acquisition, must notify its employees of the merger or acquisition. Notification must be made at least thirty days before the invitation to the GMS, to allow employees to decide whether they want to continue their employment following the transaction. In relation to an asset sale, the announcement to employees is not mandatory nevertheless in practice this is typically conducted.

[337] Employee opinion can be expressed and can have an impact on the stakeholders' decision, as if the employees are not satisfied with the planned action they have the option to resign. In terms of a major transaction, employee consent is not required. Employers who wish to dismiss employees must first obtain approval from the Industrial Relations Court. Consultation or discussion with the employee or labour union is required prior to mass or individual dismissal.

[338] Employees are entitled to be informed or consulted in relation to any other corporate transactions. However, the works council itself does not exercise any rights but serves as a body to facilitate negotiations and, in some cases, settlement of disputes depending on the terms of the Collective Labour Agreement (*'CLA'*) and applicable laws.

[339] There are no differences between blue collar workers and white collar workers in the matter of termination. Except for the board of directors or the board of commissioners that is regulated by Law No. 40/2007.

[340] Labour costs in Indonesia are regulated by the regional governor based on the council's recommendation. These councils comprise representatives from the Ministry of Manpower and Transmigration, the All Indonesia Workers' Union, employers' associations and academia. Provincial wage councils set minimum wage levels for each province and for each of the districts within the province.

[341] Unions generally have significant power to negotiate and set the minimum wage. In the matter where there is no agreement on the amount of the minimum wage, usually the Unions will conduct demonstration and labour strikes.

Pensions

[342] The Pension provision in Indonesia for companies and their employees is governed under Law No. 11 of 1992 on the Pension Fund, under which a private sector employer is not required to provide a pension plan to a worker. The requirements for the employee in order to be a participant of the pension fund according to the Law No. 11/1992 are:

(1) Every employee who is considered an employee that fulfils the requirements of being a participant, has a right to be a participant if they are at least 18 years old or married, and has had a period of employment of at least one year. It is not stated clearly regarding the requirements of being a participant, because practically it deals with the Pension Fund Regulation as stipulated by the founders and legalized by the Minister of Finance. The provision on the normal pension age shall be stipulated in the Pension Fund Regulation and it may not exceed the provision stipulated by the Minister of Manpower and Transmigration.

(2) There are two types of pension funds fees which are the employer and participant fee. If the pension funds determine the participant fee, therefore the employer shall collect the fee from the participant every month. The amount of the participant fee may not exceed the amount stipulated by the Minister of Finance.

(3) If the founders and/or their partnership cannot fulfil the obligation of paying the pension funds to the participant, then the membership of the participant may be suspended or terminated.

(4) Participants may not use the pension funds as a collateral loan, and it cannot be diverted.

[343] For any company action such as merger, acquisition, or consolidation that may impact the re-arrangement of the company management including employment, shall not affect the performance of the pension funds that already exist. Because pension funds are an independent legal entity established by the founders which consists of:

(a) Individual or entity who established the Employer Pension Fund.

(b) Bank or Insurance Company who establish the Financial Institution Pension Fund.

[344] The founders may be the employer or their partnership that employ the employee. Therefore, as long as the founders still exist in the company after the company actions, the pension funds still may conduct its activities according to their pension funds regulation. However, if there is a change of the founders, pursuant to the Law No. 11/1992, the administrator shall make changes of the pension funds regulation, or if the pension funds shall be dissolved, it may only be conducted following the permission from the Minister of Finance.

[345] Under the individual pension fund regulations, all pension contributions with interest are allocated to the employee when they resign or are dismissed. The employee cannot normally continue his contributions to the financial institution pension fund following dismissal or resignation.

Retention of Key Management and Employees

[346] It is customary that the offer letter is co-signed by the prospective purchaser who will obtain control over the management of the company, confirming or guaranteeing continued employment after closing.

Treatment of Foreign Employees

[347] Employers are prohibited from recruiting foreign workers for positions listed in the Appendix of Minister of Labor Decree No. 40 of 2012 on Occupation that are Closed to Foreign Workers, covering:

(1) Personnel Director.
(2) Industrial Relations Manager.
(3) Human Resources Manager.
(4) Personnel Development Supervisor.
(5) Personnel Recruitment Supervisor.
(6) Personnel Placement Supervisor.
(7) Employee Career development Supervisor.
(8) Human Resources Administrator.
(9) Chief Executive Officer.
(10) Personnel and Careers Specialist.
(11) Personnel Specialist.
(12) Career Advisor.
(13) Job Advisor.
(14) Job Advisor and Counselling.
(15) Employee Mediator.
(16) Job Training Administrator.
(17) Job Interviewer.
(18) Job Analyst.
(19) Occupational Safety Specialist.

[348] Minister of Manpower Regulation No. 10 of 2018 on the Procedures For Recruitment of Foreign Workers regulates foreign workers have to meet the following criteria to work in Indonesia:

(a) must possess adequate educational qualifications;
(b) must posses certificates of competence or must have working experience within the relevant business sector amounting to at least five years;

(c) must engage in the transfer of their skills to domestic co-workers;
(d) must possess an official tax payer identification (NPWP) if the foreign workers have worked in Indonesia for more than six months; and
(e) must possess valid Limited-Stay Residency Permits (ITAS).

Foreign workers are prohibited to occupy position which is in charge for human resources and/or certain positions. In addition, foreign workers may have two positions in two companies, in the following positions:

(a) Non-shareholder Director or commissioner; or
(b) Certain sectors consisting of education and vocational training sector, digital economic sector, as well as oil and gas sector for contractors who utilize cooperation contract.

[349] Every employer employing foreign employees must have a written permit from the Minister of Manpower & Transmigration namely Foreign Worker Recruitment Plan (‘*Rencana Penggunaan Tenaga Kerja Asing*’ or ‘*RPTKA*’), and from the Immigration Official namely Visa Approval Certificate; Visa Approval Certificate; Vitas; Itas; Re-entry Permit.

[350] Foreigners who reside or are present in Indonesia for more than 183 days within a single period of twelve months or who are present in Indonesia and have the intention to live in Indonesia, are required to register for a tax identity number (NPWP) and file income tax returns. This twelve-month period is based on today going back twelve months. It is not a calendar year. (The ‘intention’ to live in Indonesia is seen by such actions as applying for a work-permit, owning or renting a house for an extended period, and bringing family members to Indonesia). In addition, please be advised that, according to the law, those who must pay Indonesian income taxes if they have been here the 183 days in a calendar year, includes, those expats here on KITAS, KITAP, business visa or social/visit visas.

[351] The most significant impact of labour regulations on mergers is that they call for independent approval by the authorities to approve resulting (mass) terminations and impose obligations for payment of severance pay even in case of pure acquisitions. Based on Indonesia’s recent history, due to the political and economic crisis, unauthorized labour strikes and riots might have to be taken into consideration and must be catered for irrespective of any formal legal aspects relating to mergers and acquisitions.

[352] Law No. 13/2003 on Manpower is the governing piece of legislation on labour issues in Indonesia.

[353] In the case of labour dismissal occurring because companies are closed due to continuous losses, or force majeure, or the implementation of corporate efficiency, workers are entitled to obtain severance pay of up to twice their regular salaries, gratuities and compensations unless otherwise amicably agreed upon by both parties.

[354] Any obligation to pay severance pay, gratuity, and compensations is charged to the new employers, unless otherwise stipulated by agreements between the old and new employers.

[355] Severance pay, gratuity, and compensations must be paid in cash. The minimum amounts of severance pay are calculated as follows:

(a) working period of less than one year: one month of wage;
(b) working period of one year or more, but less than two years: two months of wage;
(c) working period of two years or more, but less than three years: three months of wage;
(d) working period of three years or more, but less than four years: four months of wage;
(e) working period of four years or more, but less than five years: five months of wage;
(f) working period of five years or more, but less than six years: six months of wage;
(g) working period of six years or more, but less than seven years: seven months of wage;
(h) working period of seven years or more, but less than eight years: eight months of wage.
(i) working period of eight years or more, nine months of wage.

[356] The minimum amounts of gratuity are as follows:

(a) working period of three years or more, but less than six years: two months of wage;
(b) working period of six years or more, but less than nine years: three months of wage;
(c) working period of nine years or more, but less than twelve years: four months of wage;
(d) working period of twelve years or more, but less than fifteen years: five months of wage;
(e) working period of fifteen years or more, but less than eighteen years: six months of wage;
(f) working period of eighteen years or more, but less than twenty-one years: seven months of wage;
(g) working period of twenty-one years or more, but less than twenty-four years: eight months of wage;
(h) working period of twenty-four years or more: ten months of wage.

[357] Compensation will include:

(a) compensation for annual leave not yet taken or not yet expired;
(b) compensation for long-service leave if applicable and the employee is determined to be eligible for long-service leave;

(c) cost or expenses for employees and their families to return to places where they take up work;
(d) compensation for housing and medical treatment can be as high as 15% of severance pay and/or gratuity if the employee is eligible;
(e) other matters as stipulated by Regional Committees or the Central Committee.

[358] Wages as the basis for payment of severance pay, gratuity, and compensations will consist of:

(a) principal wages;
(b) all kinds of fixed allowances given to workers free of charge. In the case of subsidies, the wages component is the difference between actual costs less the amount paid by the workers.

[359] In the case of workers being given wages on the basis of per unit results or commission basis, wages for one day equates to the average daily wage for the last twelve months.

[360] In the case of jobs dependent on weather conditions and wages based on contract wages, wages for one month will be calculated from the average wages earned in the last twelve months.

[361] In the case of workers receiving wages on a daily or contract basis, all of the allowances as governed by prevailing regulations which are paid by employers shall be calculated as components of wages for the basis of calculation of severance pay, gratuity and compensations.

[362] Further, in the event of acquisition, the existing Company Regulation or CLA remains valid during the term of such Company Regulation or CLA. In the event of merger, the existing company must compose a new Company Regulation within six months after the merger has taken place. Pending the legalization of such new Company Regulation, the existing Company Regulation of each of the companies will remain valid. If each of the companies to be merged and the company resulting from the merger has its own CLA, the CLA that will remain valid will be the one that is more beneficial to the employees.

[363] Of particular note is a provision of the Law No. 13/2003 that allows employees to refuse to continue their employment in the event of a change of status, merger, consolidation, or change of ownership, in which case the employees are entitled to the above-described benefits upon the termination of employment.

ACCOUNTING TREATMENT

[364] The accounting standards in Indonesia refer to the Indonesian Financial Accounting Standards ('*IFAS*' or '*PSAK*') as guidance. Deviation from the IFAS/PSAK is possible but under very limited condition in which only if the relevant regulatory framework is requires such deviation to occur or, at the minimum, does not prohibits such deviation. In addition such deviation also required to be conducted by all companies within the same industry (in which if there is a company within the same industry which does not deviates from the PSAK, then all other companies in such industry shall not deviates from the PSAK). In this case, related to the relation between the IFRS provisions and the IFAS/PSAK provision, it is known that the intended purpose of the IFRS convergence as stipulated by the International Accounting Standard Board ('*IASB*') is a full adoption of the IFRS itself, which means in this case, the IFRS convergence is purposed to make the IFAS/PSAK to be the same with the IFRS, without any modification. The adoption of IFRS in Indonesia is not conducted with 'full adoption'. There are still some modifications in the IFAS/PSAK which makes some key differences from the IFRS. Therefore, for Indonesian Companies accounting purpose, the IFRS could be implemented on the provisions where the IFAS/PSAK is in line with the IFRS. Furthermore, soon, the Indonesian companies will feel an increasing effect of IFRS as Indonesian GAAP continues to adopt IFRS.

[365] In relation to the fair values, according to the 2015 adjustment version of the PSAK 68 on Fair Value Measurement, it is determined that Fair Value is a market based measurement, not a specific measurement over an entity. For several assets and liabilities, market transaction or observable market information could be available. But, the fair value measurement objectives in both cases are the same, which is to estimate price where an orderly transaction to sell assets or transferring liabilities will occur between market participants on the measurement date from the current market condition (which is the exit price on the measurement date from the perspective of market participants which having assets or liabilities). When the price for an identical assets or liabilities could not be observed, the entity measures the fair value using other assessment technique which maximize the usage of the relevant observable inputs and minimize the usage of unobservable inputs. Because fair value is a market based measurement, therefore fair value is measured using assumption which the market participants will use when determining assets and liabilities price, including assumption on risk. As the result, the intention of the entity to own an asset or to resolve or fulfilling a liability becomes irrelevant when measuring fair value.

[366] The 2015 adjustment version of the PSAK 22 on Business Combination determine that goodwill shall no longer able to be amortized by stating that entity is obliged to suspend the amortization over goodwill since the book year period which starting on or after 1 January 2011. Therefore, an impairment test over goodwill shall be conducted based on 2014 revision of PSAK 48 on Asset Value Impairment. By the end of each reporting period, an entity shall assess whether there is an indication which an asset has undergone value impairment. If such indication exist, the entity estimates the recovered amount of such asset. More specific for Goodwill which acquired from business combination, regardless of whether there is a value impairment indication or not, the entity shall, once a year at the minimum, to conduct an impairment test by comparing the recorded value with the relieved amount. In assessing whether the asset may have experience value impairment, the entity shall consider, at the minimum, the following things:

(1) Information from external sources:
   - Significant changes of market value.
   - Significant changes of technology, market, economy, and legal scope.
   - Changes of interest rate.
   - The recorded amount of the entity's net asset exceeding its market capitalization.

(2) Information from internal sources:
   - Proof of obsolescence or physical damage to the asset.
   - Significant changes over usage, suspension, and useful lives of the asset.
   - Internal proof which indicates that the economic performance of the asset is worse than the expected.

[367] When there is an indication that there is a value impairment of an asset, the entity is required to measure the relieved amount of such asset.

[368] According to the 2015 adjustment version of the PSAK 19 on Intangible assets, in order to be able to be considered as recognized, the intangible assets shall be recognized only, and only if:

(a) There is a major possibility that the entity will gain future economic benefit from such asset.
(b) The acquisition expenses over such assets could be reliably measured.

[369] In assessing the possibility of future economic benefit existence, the entity shall use rational and accountable assumption which is the best of management's estimation over the prevailing economic condition during the benefit period of such asset. In addition, an asset could be said as identifiable if:

(a) Could be separated, that is separated or differentiated from entity and sold, moved, licensed, rented or exchanged, whether separately or jointly with the related contract, asset or indentified liability, regardless from whether the entity intended to do such thing.
(b) Arising from contract or other legal rights, regardless from whether such rights are transferable or separated from the entity or from other rights and obligations.

[370] PSAK 19 on Intangible Assets determines that, the accounting for intangible assets is based on its useful lives. An Intangible asset with limited useful lives is amortized, and an intangible asset with unlimited useful lives is not amortized. The period of amortization for intangible assets with limited useful lives should be started when the asset is available to be used, which is when the asset is located on the location and in the condition to be operational in accordance with the provision which required by the management. Amortization shall be suspended at the time which comes first between when the asset is classified as an owned assets to be sold (or is including in the removable assets which is categorized as an owned asset to be sold) in accordance with the 2014 adjustment version of the PSAK 58 on Long

Term Assets Which Owned To Be Sold And The Suspended Operation and the date when the recognition over such asset is suspended. For Intangible Assets with unlimited useful lives, PSAK 19 determine that an intangible asset with unlimited useful lives shall not be amortized, and an entity is required to test an intangible asset with unlimited useful lives for value impairment with comparing the relieved amount with the recorded amount:

(a) Every year.
(b) At any time when there is an indication that the intangible assets is experiencing value impairment.

[371] According to PSAK 22 on Business Combination, negative goodwill will need to be credited to the profit and loss account. It will be recorded on the credit side as profit account resulting from business combination.

[372] According to PSAK 22 on Business Combination, paragraph [53] states that acquisition related costs is the cost incurred by the acquiring party in the framework of business combination. Moreover, paragraph [53] states that the acquiring party is obliged to record the acquisition related costs as a liability on the period by the time such cost occurred and the services is received, with one exception, which is the cost to issue bonds and equity, where it shall be recognized in accordance with the 2015 adjustment version of the PSAK 55 on Financial Instrument: Recognition and Measurement and the 2014 adjustment version of the PSAK 50 on Financial Instrument: Presentation and Disclosure. In general, acquisition costs shall be imposed to the profit and loss statement on the period when such cost occurred.

[373] Regarding the effective date of an acquisition framework in Indonesia, it is governed on PSAK 22 on Business Combination. Such provision stated that the acquiring party identifies the acquisition date, which is the date when the acquiring party gain control over the acquired party. In general, the date when the acquiring party gain control over the acquired party is the date when the acquiring party, by virtue of the law, transfers the reward, acquire the asset, and takes over the liabilities of the acquired party, which is the closing date. However, the acquiring party may gain control before or after the closing date. For instance, the acquisition date precedes the closing date if in a written agreement it is stated that the acquiring party gains control over the acquired party on the date before the closing date. The acquiring party considers all the related facts and conditions in determining the acquisition date.

[374] Indonesian accounting principles on the effect of mergers and acquisitions do not necessarily coincide with the tax treatment or legal treatment of the particular merger or acquisition. In the worst-case scenario, each of the respective disciplines will treat each merger or acquisition differently.

[375] Indonesian principles of accounting provide the following definitions:

(a) A *merger* is the merger of two or more separate companies into one economic entity as one company unites with another or takes control of the assets and operations of the other company.

(b) An *acquisition* is a merger in which one of the companies, namely the acquirer, takes control over the net assets and operations of the acquired company or acquiree by giving particular assets, acknowledging liability or issuing shares.
(c) A *uniting of interests/pooling of interests* is a merger in which shareholders of the merging company jointly take control over all matters, or effectively all net assets and operations of the merging company and, further, jointly assume any risks and benefits attached to the merging entity, so that no party may be identified as acquiring company or acquirer.
(d) A *holding company* is a company having one or more subsidiaries.
(e) A *subsidiary company* is a company controlled by another company (known as the holding company).
(f) A *minority interest* is part of the proceeds and net assets of the company not owned directly or indirectly through subsidiaries by the holding company.
(g) *Fair value* is an amount used as the basis of assets exchange or fulfilment of liabilities between any knowledgeable party and any party willing to conduct an arm's length transaction.
(h) *Transaction date* is the date when control over the net assets and operations of the acquiree is effectively transferred to the acquirer.

Merger

[376] A merger may be conducted in many ways based on legal considerations, taxes or for other reasons. In the principles of accounting, merger has several definitions, as follows:

(a) A merger may be in the form of a purchase of shares in a company by another company or the purchase of net assets of a company.
(b) A merger may be conducted by issuing shares or delivering cash, assets equivalent to cash or other assets, or transactions made between shareholders of the merging company or between a company and shareholders of the other company.
(c) A merger may be in the form of establishment of a new company to control the merging company, and the transfer of net assets of one or more merging companies to the other company or winding up of one or more merging companies.

[377] In the event of a merging company being a member of a group of companies, or part of several groups of companies, the merger plan must include the consolidated balance sheet as well as the pro forma balance sheet of the resulting merger.

[378] A merger may cause a legal merger, which usually is a merger of two companies through one of the following procedures:

(a) assets and liabilities of a company are transferred to another company and the transferring company is dissolved; or

(b) assets and liabilities of two or more companies are transferred to a new company and both transferring companies are dissolved.

[379] Basically, there are differences between the definition of a merger from a legal and an accounting point of view. Principles of accounting regard legal merger in two circumstances as mentioned above, but from a legal point of view, merger is merely as defined in (a) below, while (b) below is a consolidation. Article 1 of GR No. 27/1998 states as follows:

(a) Merger is legal action conducted by one or more companies to merge with another existing company and, furthermore, the merging company is dissolved.
(b) Consolidation is legal action conducted by two or more companies to consolidate by establishing a new company and each consolidating company is dissolved.

[380] From a legal point of view, both circumstances described above involve two different concepts and legal consequences.

Acquisition

[381] Merger through acquisition must be recorded by using the purchase method. The use of the purchase method for the acquisition of a company is recorded as the purchase of other assets. This is performed in an acquisition where there is a transfer of assets, liabilities or a shares issue in order to take control over the net assets and operations of another company. The purchase method uses the cost of acquisition as a basis to record the acquisition. As of the acquisition date, namely the date when control over the assets and operations of an acquired company (acquiree) is effectively transferred to the acquirer and the date when the application of purchase method is commenced, the acquiring company must:

(a) report the proceeds of the acquiring company in its profit and loss statement; and
(b) report the assets and liabilities of the acquired company in its balance sheet and any goodwill resulting from the acquisition.

[382] An acquisition must be recorded as the cost of acquisition, namely the amount of cash or assets equivalent to cash paid or fair value (on the exchange date) of other assets provided by the acquiring company as payment for the acquisition of control over the net assets of the other company, plus other costs directly attributed to the acquisition.

[383] If, in an acquisition, there is more than one transaction, the cost of acquisition is the total sum of all transactions. If an acquisition is conducted gradually, the difference between the acquisition date and transaction date is very important. Since acquisition from an accounting point of view is commenced as from the acquisition date, information relating to the acquiring cost and fair value set out at every transaction date will be used.

[384] Basically, in all mergers, one of the merging companies takes control over another company. Control is assumed to be taken if one of the merging companies receives more than 50% of the voting rights in another company, unless it is established that no company controls or has ownership of more than 50%. Although one of the merging companies does not have more than 50% voting rights, the acquiring company may nevertheless be identified when one of the merging companies obtains the following:

(a) control of more than 50% votes over such other company is based on an agreement with another investor;
(b) the power to change the financial policy and operation of such other company is based on the articles of association or agreement;
(c) power to designate and dismiss part of the board of directors of such other company;
(d) power to obtain majority votes in the meeting of the board of directors in such other company.

[385] Although it is occasionally difficult to identify the acquiring company, there is a way to determine the acquirer, for instance:

(a) the fair value of the merging company is significantly larger than such other company. In this regard, such company is an acquirer;
(b) integration of business activities is implemented through the exchange of voting common shares for corporate current assets. In this case, such company shall be an acquiree; or
(c) a merger results in the management of a company having the ability to dominate the appointment of the board of directors of the merging company. In this case, such dominating company is an acquirer.

[386] A company can obtain shares in another company, but, as a part of the exchange transaction, such company issues its voting shares in an amount that results in control over the merging company being transferred to the shareholders of the company whose shares are being acquired. This acquisition is called *reverse acquisition*. Although the company issuing the shares is formally declared as the mother company, the acquiring company that is the shareholders that now have control over the company resulting from the merger, will enjoy the benefits of such voting rights or other rights. The company issuing such shares is considered as having been acquired by the other merging company, and such other company is considered as the acquired company. Therefore, the purchasing of assets and liabilities method of the company issuing such shares must be applied.

[387] GR No. 27/1998 on Merger, Consolidation, and Acquisition of PT states in Article 1 of Law No. 40/2007 that acquisition is a legal action conducted by a legal entity or an individual to take over all or part of the shares of a company that may result in the transfer of control of the company. Article 37 of Law No. 40/2007 states:

> A company may repurchase a share which has been issued, provided that:
>
> (a) it is paid for by net profits as long as such payment does not cause the company's net assets to become less than the aggregate of the amount of issued capital plus the statutory reserve which is obligatory in accordance with the provisions of this Law; and
> (b) the aggregate sum of the nominal value of all shares owned by the company together with the shares owned by its subsidiaries, and the pledged shares which are held by it, does not exceed 10% of the amount of its issued capital.

[388] An acquisition must be accounted at the amount of income cost, which is the total of cash on hand or assets equivalent to cash that have been paid or fair value (on the date of exchange) of other assets provided for by the acquiring company in exchange for obtaining control of the acquired company, plus other expenses directly attributed to the aforesaid acquisition. In determining income, securities issued by the acquired company must be evaluated based on fair value, namely market price, at the date of the exchange transaction. The general guidelines in determining the fair value of the assets and liabilities to be acquired are as follows:

(a) marketable securities are based on prevailing market value;
(b) non-marketable securities will be estimated based on the price earnings ratio, dividends, and expected growth of companies with similar characteristics;
(c) accounts receivable will be determined by the present value and applicable interest rates, less reserves for possible non-collectable receivables and costs of collection under prevailing conditions. However, short-term receivables must not necessarily apply any deductions if the difference between nominal value and present value is immaterial;
(d) supply:
  (i) finished goods and trading goods will be valued at selling price less: (a) cost of disposal; and (b) assumed fair profit that is established on the basis of profit margins of similar products;
  (ii) unfinished goods are valued at the selling price of finished goods less: (a) cost of finishing; and (b) the selling cost based on profit margins of similar goods;
  (iii) raw materials are valued based on current replacement cost.
(e) land and buildings:
  (i) if utilized in accordance with its original intentions, will be valued at the market price of the said utilization;
  (ii) if utilized differently than its original intentions, will be valued on the basis of market prices of expected utilization intentions;
  (iii) if to be sold or temporarily withheld and later to be resold, will be valued at net realizable value.
(f) plant and equipment:

(i) if utilized, will be valued at market prices established by an appraisal company. In the event that the market value is difficult to establish due to the plant and equipment having a special character, the calculation will be based on depreciated replacement cost;

(ii) if to be utilized temporarily, the net realizable value will be applied.

(g) intangible assets such as patents and licenses, will be valued on the basis of appraisal;

(h) net assets or liabilities of definite pension benefits, are established on the basis of the present actuarial value of the pension benefits promised, less the fair asset value made available for the pension program;

(i) collectables and tax liabilities are established in accordance with applicable tax laws in respect of mergers;

(j) accounts payable, cheques, long-term debt, liabilities, accrued and other debts will be based on present value, less applicable fair discount prevailing at that time;

(k) liabilities in relation to a plant closure and termination of contract due to acquisition, will be appraised at present value payable at discounted rate in accordance with prevailing fair interest rates.

[389] Several of the above-mentioned guidelines assume that fair value will be established by applying discounts. However, such discounts are not obligatory in the establishment of fair asset value and identifiable liabilities.

[390] In accordance with accounting principles, an acquisition must be valued at its purchase price, which is established by the value of the cash paid and/or other assets transferred at the fair market value of the acquiring company, plus other expenses directly attributed to the acquisition. Prevailing tax laws however stipulate that book value of the resulting merger or acquisition may be applied for tax purposes, subject to approval by the Directorate General of Taxation. Such approval may only be considered after all outstanding taxes of all legal entities are merged or acquired.

[391] The merger and acquisition process may have different meanings, treatment, and arrangement, depending on whether seen from an accounting or legal perspective. Such differences can be disadvantageous for business activities and practitioners as they can cause uncertainty.

FUTURE DEVELOPMENTS

[392] The current Negative Investment List PR No. 44/2016, would be revised shortly.

[393] Specific changes that are currently expected include restrictions on foreign ownership in banks where the limit is expected to be reduced to 51% from the current 99%.

[394] Other significant legislative revisions that are expected are:

- A new Banking Law, which would set out the foreign ownership limit mentioned above, and is also expected to require all insurance companies, banks, and foreign branches, to incorporate in the form of PT.
- A new **Prohibition of Monopolistic Practice and Unfair Business Competition Law, which would broaden the authority of** the Commission for the Supervision of Business Competition (*Komisi Pengawas Persaingan Usaha* (KPPU)).
- In addition, two other related draft bills are also currently being prepared for future deliberation by the Minister, specifically: (1) The Draft Bill on Fiduciary Security (*Jaminan Fidusia*); and (2) The Draft Bill on Bankruptcy.

Made in the USA
Monee, IL
18 October 2026

66036822R00063